It's A Team Game

Scottish Football Club Line-Ups In The Black & White Era

By Steve Finan

ISBN 978-1-84535-794-8

First published in Great Britain in 2019 by DC Thomson & Co., Ltd.,
Meadowside, Dundee, DD1 9QJ
Copyright © DC Thomson & Co., Limited.

Visit **www.dcthomsonshop.co.uk**
To purchase this book.
Or Freephone 0800 318 846 / Overseas customers call +44 1382 575580
Typeset & internal design by Steve Finan.

This book is set in Times New Roman standard/bold 14pt on 16.8 leading.

Cover design by Leon Strachan.

■ **Zoltan Varga (front, right) exchanges banter with his Aberdeen 1973 team-mates.**

It's A Team Game

Scottish Football Club Line-Ups In The Black & White Era

By Steve Finan

For all those who have ever played professional football. It isn't an easy game, no matter what it looks like. Every man who ever made it into a senior team, or even the fringes, was among the top 0.01% of footballers. A hero. Their talents deserve respect, each and every one of them.

This book is dedicated to Theo Ray Nicoll.

■ This page: Inverness Thistle right-back Roshie Fraser married Dolina Nicolson on October 9th, 1970, but delayed his honeymoon so he could take the field against Clachnacuddin at Telford Street Park on the Saturday, October 10th. Thistle won 6-1, and here Roshie and his wife hold the Highland League Cup after the match.

■ Front cover: Motherwell FC 1969-70 (see page 146).

Introduction

SCOTTISH FOOTBALL'S great players and managers have praise heaped upon them. Their exploits are the stuff of fable, their names are wreathed in legend.

But every footballer who ever walked on to a pitch did so as part of a team.

This book seeks to celebrate individual footballers, famous games, great achievements and some of the game's truths and oddities. It does so by showing the teams involved.

If you are a football fan, when you read through the line-ups you'll recognise some players, but perhaps will have forgotten others.

These photos have lain in newspaper and magazine archives for decades. Some are tattered round the edges. Some are badly damaged. Some don't quite have complete left-to-right captions.

These photographs have had long working lives. There are crop marks where editors wanted cuts made or had demanded head-and-shoulder shots of individual players. Some have had the background removed. Some have been re-touched. They were in use in the pre-digital age, when photo manipulation was done with chinagraph pencils and sprayguns.

I make no apology for any of that. These heirloom photos bear the scars of their existence in the history of newspaper and magazine production.

The content of the photos, however, is young men in their prime and in their natural element. Often you can see the horseplay, banter and words spoken out the corners of mouths.

Their vitality and youth is captured and frozen for ever.

The men themselves, of course, aged, greyed and in many cases died long ago. But these photos show the way they were when they were full of vigour and eager to play the game they loved.

It is not a complete record of every team's great achievements, nor does it show every great player who ever graced the game.

Not even close.

Some of the teams and players weren't ever champions or cup winners. Some weren't even very good. But football is for everyone, not just the most skilled and not just for teams that win trophies.

I proudly display teams that might not be in any other collection of photos. Some of the men picked out might not have been regarded as their team's stars.

But every star player needed a team to play in, and every team member had a part to play.

If a book that celebrates teams can do anything at all, it can showcase a few players who didn't stand out, didn't shine, but contributed to the whole.

It has always been a team game.

Steve Finan

■ Alex Stott and George "Pud" Hill of Dundee FC, 1949.

I'll have strayed offside . . .

THERE are gaps in the record of players at some, if not all, clubs. Names weren't kept, names weren't accurately collected by photographers, sometimes names weren't even known.

I fulsomely apologise for this.

Even the most complete archives of trialists, reserves, guests and youngsters don't have all the names of all the players who somehow found their way into pre-season line-ups.

Sometimes they will have been trialists or kids who never progressed beyond the "shows promise" stage and disappeared from the game altogether, their names going with them.

In some cases, the players may have gone on to have fine careers but with other clubs, some may have rejoined the Junior ranks.

Some players will be missing from photos they should be in for reasons that will seem strange now, but made perfect sense at the time.

For instance, Freddie Glidden isn't in the 1958 Hearts record-setting line-up on page 84. The reason is he couldn't get time off work. Glidden was an integral part of that team at right-half, but also had a good job with West Lothian Water Board.

Sometimes spellings might be incorrect. On other occasions, names (or at least full names) proved impossible for me to discover, though they might be obvious to a supporter, or common knowledge among the records-keepers of clubs.

Every club has a few dedicated fans like this, with priceless information kept in ledgers or hard drives in the privacy of their own home.

I crave forgiveness for any wrong information or incomplete information. All errors should be regarded as my errors.

Indeed, there will probably be mistakes that I shouldn't have allowed to pass and, again, I can only apologise.

I would ask that if you have better, more accurate, info than I could find, then please get in touch to correct me and enlighten me — I'll be very grateful as I'd hope to include updated and corrected captions in future pressings or editions of this book.

Lastly, I thoroughly enjoyed compiling this book. My heart was gladdened to find references to players I had long forgotten. It was like seeing old friends.

My one hope is that anyone who ever reads this book has a similar experience.

Steve Finan
sfinan@dctmedia.co.uk

■ **Hearts in beach training 1960: From left: Young, Murray, Oliver.**

Thanks to...The Team

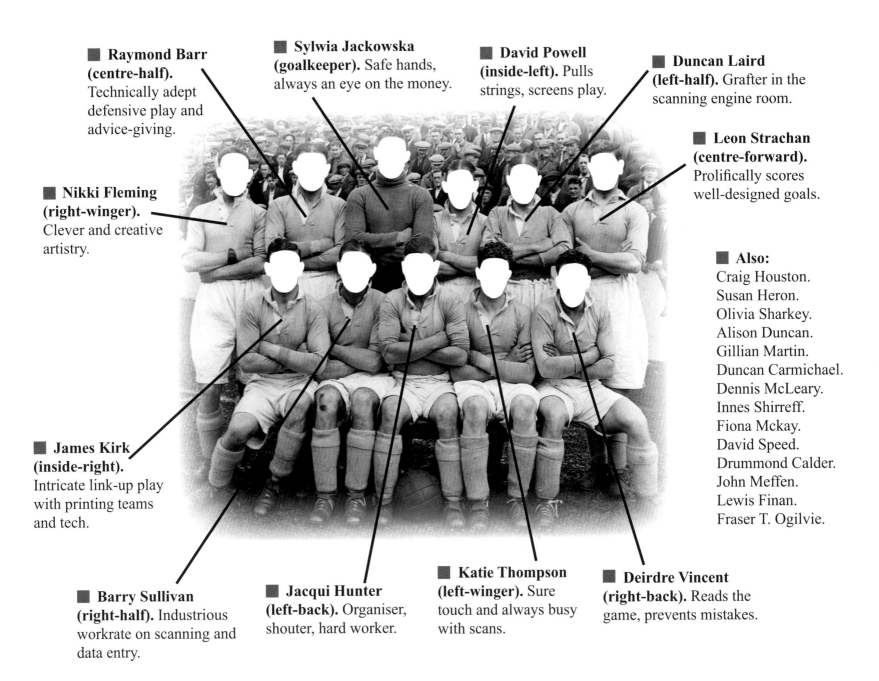

Raymond Barr (centre-half). Technically adept defensive play and advice-giving.

Sylwia Jackowska (goalkeeper). Safe hands, always an eye on the money.

David Powell (inside-left). Pulls strings, screens play.

Duncan Laird (left-half). Grafter in the scanning engine room.

Leon Strachan (centre-forward). Prolifically scores well-designed goals.

Nikki Fleming (right-winger). Clever and creative artistry.

James Kirk (inside-right). Intricate link-up play with printing teams and tech.

Barry Sullivan (right-half). Industrious workrate on scanning and data entry.

Jacqui Hunter (left-back). Organiser, shouter, hard worker.

Katie Thompson (left-winger). Sure touch and always busy with scans.

Deirdre Vincent (right-back). Reads the game, prevents mistakes.

Also:
Craig Houston.
Susan Heron.
Olivia Sharkey.
Alison Duncan.
Gillian Martin.
Duncan Carmichael.
Dennis McLeary.
Innes Shirreff.
Fiona Mckay.
David Speed.
Drummond Calder.
John Meffen.
Lewis Finan.
Fraser T. Ogilvie.

1885~Greatest team of all time

WHO could argue? The 36-0 Arbroath FC team of September 12, 1885, recorded the biggest winning margin in world football history. Doesn't that make them the best team this planet has ever seen?

On the same day, Dundee Harp beat Aberdeen Rovers 35-0. Football reporting was in its infancy but the Manchester-based *Athletic News*, a sports weekly of the time, recognised these achievements.

The paper wrote, "There was a terrible slaughtering of the innocents of Aberdeen on Saturday. Between them, the Bon Accord and Rovers lost 71 goals, the one 36 and the other 35. Arbroath defeated the Bon Accord, and the Rovers fell without a murmur to the Harp.

"Arbroath have thus the honour of establishing a record, so far as goal-taking is concerned. Aberdeen, from these figures, is evidently low in football. Saturday's work will for ever stand against them."

The Dundee Courier of Tuesday, September 15, 1885 reported the Arbroath game as: "EXTRAORDINARY FARCE. This match was played at Arbroath on Saturday, when, despite the rain, there was a good turn-out of spectators.

"The match was one of the drollest ever seen here or anywhere else, and baffles description. It was truly the 'Massacre of the Innocents' for a more helpless set of innocents never before met the crack club of Forfarshire.

"Though unable to describe the match, we can give the result, which we hope no one will doubt. Two forty-fives were played. The first was Arbroath 15; Bon-Accord 0; second — Arbroath, 21; Bon-Accord, 0. Grand total Arbroath 36 ; Bon Accord 0.

"Milne, the goalkeeper of the Arbroath, neither touched the ball with hand or foot during the match, but remained under the friendly shelter of an umbrella the whole time."

And so the result passed into history, and history became legend.

The best team of all time.

■ **The record-setting Arbroath team. Sitting behind the ball is outside-right Jockie Petrie, who scored 13 of the goals.**

1910~And never again

THERE is no such thing as a curse, or a hex. Football is a game in which skill and endeavour are what count. Luck plays a part, but a goalkeeper making a good save isn't luck, and a striker shooting past the post isn't luck either. Those are flashes of brilliance or mistakes, luck doesn't enter into it. So whatever it is that wins or loses championships and cups, it isn't voodoo or witch-women or the casting of spells.

But folklore in the city of Dundee has strange tales to tell.

One version has it that when the 1910 Dundee FC Scottish Cup-winning team arrived home by train, a gypsy woman was roughly jostled by the jubilant crowd. Another account has it that the cup was displayed in the window of an undertaker, and a local "wise woman" (a term basically meaning "witch") was incensed by this disrespect for the dead.

Both tales end the same way. A curse was then uttered, the woman cried: "1910 and never again", meaning Dundee would never again bring home the cup.

Nonsense.

But Dundee haven't won the Scottish Cup since that day.

They have had good teams, winning the Championship and three times capturing the League Cup, but the Scottish Cup has never returned to Dens Park despite the Dark Blues making it to the final a further four times.

The law of averages dictates that Dundee are due a cup win soon.

■ **Dundee FC's 1910 cup winning team (second replay) was: (not in order in this photo) Bob Crumley, Bert Neal, Bob McEwan, Bert Lee, Herbert Dainty, George Comrie, Jimmy Bellamy, George Langlands, Sailor Hunter, Sandy MacFarlane, Jack Fraser. Jimmy Lawson played in the first final; John Chaplin played in the first replay. Manager was William Wallace.**

1921~Napoleon just got better with age

JIMMY McMENEMY had already had a highly successful 18-year career with Celtic — his nickname being Napoleon — before moving on to Partick Thistle in 1920.

He had won 11 league championships and six Scottish Cups, but the little inside-left was a winner to his core so playing for a new team could be no different for him. He led The Jags to their first, and so far last, Scottish Cup triumph in 1921, at the remarkable age of 41.

Because two replays in each game were required to get past Hibs, Motherwell, and then Hearts, Thistle had to play 11 games to win the cup. In the final, however, a single game and a single goal (by John Blair) was enough to beat Rangers — the goal being scored when Rangers were down to 10 men as Jimmy Bowie had left the field to change his torn shorts.

■ **Back, from left: Hamilton, Thomas Crichton, Kenneth Campbell, Jimmy McMenemy, Matthew Wilson, John Bowie, Walter Borthwick. Middle: David Johnstone, James Kinloch, Joseph Harris, Willie Bullock, Jimmy McMullan, Robert McFarlane. Front: John Blair, William Salisbury.**

1921~ Hearts

A TATTERED, but still legible, early shot of Hearts.

■ Back, from left: J. Murphy (asst. trainer), W. Brown (director), R. Gibb (groundsman), Cameron, C. Dand, Durning (trainer), R. Dunsmuir. Middle: Willie McCartney (secy & manager), Jock Gilfillan, John McRoberts, Davidson, G. Whyte, William Penman, Freddie Forbes, Makle, Jack Sharp, David Sharp, John Murphy. Front: Tom Miller, Robert Lister, McCallen, George Forrest, Bob Preston, R. Burrell, Paddy Crossan, Harry Smillie, Alex Kane, J. Miller. On ground: Jock Ramage, Jock Wilson.

■ **This Albion Rovers 1921 photo has survived a century of use. Trainer C. Thomas, Daniel Melville, Gavin Watson, David Duncan, Bill Ribchester, Andrew Ford, James Blue, Wallace, Joseph Short, Marsh, Robert Penman, Bill Hillhouse.**

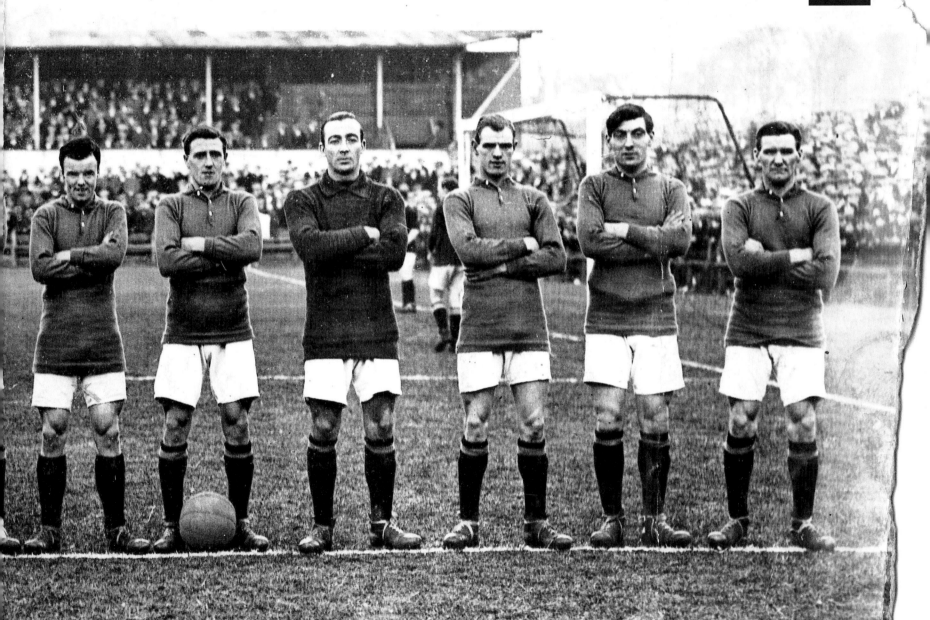

1922~A cup for the hard men of Morton

"A GAME almost devoid of artistry". "The spirit of fair play did not enter much into this struggle". "Men were laid low with an abandon and recklessness I have never seen equalled" . . . the 1922 Scottish Cup Final, a 1-0 victory for Morton over Rangers, was one of the tougher games in an era when hard men played the game.

Anyone who ever played football at a competetive level in Scotland will have been involved in this sort of game. It's a lie to pretend that it's always all about skill, geometric patterns of passing and cavalier forays forward.

Sometimes it's about winning the battle before winning the game. It's about grit. It's about getting stuck in.

It's a part of the Scottish game, or at least it used to be.

The cup went to the tail o' the bank. Morton won a hard victory in a hard game and can be proud of that.

It's the result that counts.

■ **Morton 1921-1922. Back, from left: D. Campbell (director), Jimmy Gourlay, Bob McGregor, John Stewart Wright, Jock McIntyre, Davie Edwards, Robert Brown, W. Allan, H. Howatt. Middle: R. G. Adam, Bobby McKay, John Buchanan, ex-provost W. B. McMillan, C.B.E., George French, Alfred Brown, Bob Cochran (manager), Front: Alex McNab, James McMinn.**

1924~The world's best player

WHEN the all-time greats of the game are discussed, opinion favours latter-day stars, forgetting the pre-TV era. It is this, and only this, that prevents Hughie Gallacher being hailed as perhaps the best player ever to kick a fitba.

Hughie, at 5 foot 5 inches, was a phenomenon, the Maradona of his day. His controlling touch has probably never been bettered. He carried an aura, off field as well as on, that dominated those around him.

One of the 1928 Wembley Wizards, he scored 24 goals in 20 internationals and is still Scotland's third highest scorer, nearly 90 years after his last goal.

His club career was littered with goals. In Scotland he started with QoS, then won the Cup at Airdrie, before becoming a folk hero at Newcastle. He scored 143 goals in 174 competitive games for The Toon and captained them to the 1926-27 First Division title, despite the savage attentions of defenders of the era.

His name is a Tyneside legend.

He was brilliant and he knew it, acted up to his reputation, pulled off amazing feats of football artistry, and yet delivered, year after year. Goals in threes, fours and fives. Goals from all angles and of all types.

However, his death is a sad tale. His wife passed away in 1950, of a heart condition, leaving Hughie with three sons. He had a succession of jobs to support his family, but never managed to stick at one.

One evening in 1957 at his Newcastle home Hughie threw an ashtray, hitting his 14-year-old son Matt on the head and drawing blood. The police became involved and Hughie was charged with assault.

Fearing the looming court case and the publicity it would bring, and banned from seeing Matt, he grew increasingly irrational. He walked the streets muttering, inconsolable at the guilt of hurting his son.

On June 11, 1957, the day before the case was to call, Hughie was seen on a bridge over the main Edinburgh-London railway. He was weeping, walking up and down and pounding his fists on the bridge rail.

He walked in front of an express train.

■ **A damaged shot of Airdrie, 1924. Back, from left: trainer G. Carrol, Willie Neil, Bob McPhail, Jock McDougall, Jock Ewart, Tom Preston, D. Gordon, Jimmy Allan, John Murdoch, W. Reid. Front: Jimmy Sommerville, James Reid, Willie Russell, Hughie Gallagher, George McQueen, Sandy Dick, Bob Bennie, Jimmy Howieson.**

23

1926~Always 2-3-5

STICKING with Airdrie, Hughie Gallacher thrived in the formation The Diamonds, and also Newcastle United, played.

Until the 1930s, and in some cases far beyond, the accepted wisdom was that football was played with two full-backs, three half-backs and five forwards. It was known as the pyramid system.

This morphed into the "WM", a flexible 3-2-2-3 demonstrated by the all-conquering Arsenal team of the 1930s, where the two inside-forwards dropped further back and the centre-half played level with the full-backs. Partly, this was because the offside rule changed in the mid-1920s so that strikers had to ensure that only two, not the previous three, men were between them and the goal when they received the ball.

The clever Hungarians of the 1950s brought in the WW, a

2-3-1-4 that became 2-3-2-3 when they lost the ball.

Tactics took off from there. It is now a branch of science which studies the new and re-examines greats such as the "total football" Dutch of the 1970s, and Pep Guardiola's innovative (and also retro) use of a libero in a 4-3-3, among many other systems

We still use the terminology,

though. We talk of full-backs, centre-halves and left-wingers, though how the players operate on the field is far from the old ways.

The Airdrieonians of the inter-war years lined up as a rigid 2-3-5. And they were very good at it, finishing 2nd in the league four years in a row, 1922-23 to 1925-26, and winning the Scottish Cup of 1924.

■ **The Airdrie side of 1926, lining up as a 2-3-5. Far left: full-backs Thomas Calder and Sandy Dick, with goalie Jock Ewart. Middle: half-backs Tom Preston, Jock McDougall and Archie Scott. Above: forwards James Reid, Willie Neil, Tony Weldon, Bob McPhail (soon to leave for Rangers), and Jimmy Sommerville.**

1928~Foreign jaunts

SCOTTISH football clubs have a lengthy history, even in the game's early days, of setting off on summer tours overseas — and spreading the famous "Scottish passing game".

Rangers and Celtic ventured to the Continent in the summer of 1904, both visiting Vienna and both giving the local clubs, and other touring sides, a series of football lessons with 8-0 and 6-1 beatings.

Third Lanark visited Argentina and Uruguay in 1923, before Motherwell undertook quite remarkable journeys in 1927 and 1928.

The Steelmen showed the world how the game should be played.

They won the King of Spain's Cup and Barcelona Cup in Spain in 1927, beating Real Madrid, Athletic Bilbao and Celta Vigo along the way, as well as two victories over Swansea Town who were also visiting.

In 1928 they went even further afield to South America, taking on Boca Juniors and Penarol, as well as combined Argentina-Uruguay and Brazilian selects. The '28 tour saw them away from home for around two months, playing in the stadiums of River Plate, Racing Club, Fluminense and Sao Paulo.

■ **Motherwell 1928, with the Lanarkshire Cup, the King of Spain's Cup and the Barcelona Cup. Back, from left: A. Donaldson (assist. trainer), David Hutchison, Willie McFadyen, John Johnman, Alan McClory, David Thackeray, Allan Craig, Dick Little, W. Walker (trainer). Front: Tom Tennant, James Keenan, Andrew McMurtie, John Hunter (manager), Bobby Ferrier, George Stevenson, James Bryers, Willie Tennant.**

27

1929~Bill Struth

MANY of the proud traditions of Rangers Football Club are founded upon the indomitable will of one man — Bill Struth, the most successful manager in the Scottish game. He won 18 championships, 10 Scottish Cups and two League Cups.

Struth transcended football and came to represent an ideal. Players, indeed all representatives of Rangers, were to conduct themselves in a gentlemanly manner. There are tales of Struth disapproving of his players being seen on the street with hands in pockets. Above all, however, his players had to win.

Struth knew his team would be challenged, and welcomed that. But expected his players to defeat all and any opponents who came forward..

He insisted that a fierce pride must be felt by any man pulling on a Rangers shirt, and that this pride be demonstrated in one way — with victory.

■ **Left: Bill Struth's portrait in the Rangers Trophy Room in 1959.**

■ Rangers 1929-30. J. Kerr (trainer), Davie Meiklejohn, Jim Marshall, Sandy Archibald, Jimmy Fleming, Tommy Hamilton, John Buchanan, Tommy Craig, Bill Struth. Front: George Brown, Dougie Gray, Robert McDonald, Tommy Muirhead, Bob McPhail, Bob Hamilton, W.G. Nicholson, Alan Morton.

1930~Cowdenbeath's version of Sir Alex

S IR Alex Ferguson wasn't the first high-performing Scottish manager lured south by Manchester United.

In the 1920s and '30s Scott Duncan was one of the new breed of football bosses. He had been a player at the top level for Dumbarton, Newcastle United and Rangers. He became the Hamilton Accies, then (very successfully) the Cowdenbeath manager.

Previously, managers hadn't been players. Indeed, they were often termed secretaries and some clubs' team selections were made by the directors.

But ex-players like Duncan, with their inside knowledge of playing the game, and their conspicuous success, began a new chapter in management.

Duncan became 'Beath boss in 1925 and stayed for seven years. He kept the club in the top division for the longest period in their history, finishing 5th, 7th, 7th, 13th, 16th, 7th and 12th, before the Old Trafford giants came calling in 1932.

■ **Right: Scott Duncan at Central Park. Left, some of his players at Cowdenbeath in 1930 including (sadly, not in order) Hamill, Frame, Haggerty, Black, Patterson, Anderson, Martin, Russell, Glancy, and Campbell.**

1932~East Stirlingshire are Second Division champions

IT'S not been easy being an East Stirlingshire supporter over the years. The Falkirk-based side were formed in 1881 and have spent two seasons in Scottish football's top division, 1932-33 and 1963-64.

The '32-33 campaign was a bottom-placed finish with 17 points and 117 goals conceded. The '63-64 season yielded only 12 points, but the goals-against tally that year was only 91.

Unlike Cowdenbeath on the previous page, the club didn't have an official manager until Lawrence Binnie in 1966. For the previous 85 years, the directors picked the team.

A bizarre strips malfunction brought some fame in 1998-99. Shire had signed a deal with Le Coq Sportif. But the French company failed to supply kits in time for the start of the season.

Instead, they sent a set of Queen's Park kits, with the East Stirling club badge and sponsor as ironed-on transfers on top of the QP crest.

In 2016 The Shire became the first club to be relegated out of the Scottish national league system.

Finishing bottom of League Two they met the winners of the Lowland/Highland League play-off, Edinburgh City, in a two-legged decider. The capital city side won 2-1 on aggregate.

However, The Shire have national silverware to their name.

They won the old Second Division in 1931-32. It was a tight league, with Shire and St Johnstone finishing on 55 points apiece, but the Falkirk side's goal average of 2.018 was better than the Perth club's 1.962. This is the team that won that league title.

■ **Back, from left: Thomas Copland, Edwin Powell, James Niven, Willie Fraser, Jim McCabe, Willie Crichton. Front: Johnny Latimer, William McMillan, Johnny Renwick, Jimmy Turnbull, Rabbie Kemp.**

1932~Sailor Hunter's 'Well

MANY are the legends told of Motherwell's 1931-32 league-winning side.

Bobby Ferrier's 30 goals while playing as a winger, Willie McFadyen's 52-goal haul, Welsh full-back Ben Ellis as hard as any steel produced in the town's foundries, and the cultured Alan Craig forever unruffled at centre-half. The Steelmen did, indeed, have quite a team.

They won the league at a canter, five points clear of Rangers (in those two-points-for-a-win days) and 18 points ahead of third-placed Celtic.

Motherwell were the first non-Old Firm Team to take a league championship, since Third Lanark's 1904 triumph, and no club other than Glasgow's big two would win it again until Hibs in 1948. Motherwell's achievement was a beacon of hope for other clubs.

But great though the players were, much of the credit must go to manager John "Sailor" Hunter.

Sailor, nicknamed for his rolling gait, had quite a playing career. He'd been in the first Liverpool side to win a league championship in 1900-01 and also played, with distinction, for Arsenal and Portsmouth. He had been an integral part of the Dundee team that won the 1910 Scottish Cup, scoring in the first final and then getting the winner in the second replay.

It was his signing policy at Motherwell, however, that was really clever. Managers in the future would plunder foreign markets for players, but this wasn't really possible in the 1920s. What Hunter did was scout the best young players from the Junior game and mould them into a senior league team.

It worked superbly well.

So well, in fact, that Hunter's dynamic, free-scoring team didn't just win the league, they won it in style.

■ **Motherwell FC, 1931-32. Back, from left: Willie Dowall, Allan Craig, Allan McClory, William Telfer, Hughie Wales** (who looks suspiciously like he might have been cut in to the original photo later)**, Benjamin Ellis, Willie Moffat. Front, left to right: Johnny Murdoch, John McMenemy, Bobby Ferrier, Willie McFadyen, George Stevenson.**

1933~Joe Tulip tiptoes in

JOE TULIP was among the first Englishmen to play in Scottish football. His story is one that isn't often paralleled in the modern game.

Joe was born in Mickley, Northumberland, and had trials at Blackburn Rovers in his youth but wasn't taken on. In 1933 he was playing district football in the Tyne & Wear village of Crawcrook when, legend has it, a policeman on holiday from Dumfries saw him in a game.

The policeman went home and recommended Joe to Queen of the South. After a trial, the stocky winger moved north and starred for Queens in the years when they were a top-division side.

He was a firm favourite with the Palmerston crowd and his good form is said to have drawn interest from Wolverhampton Wanderers and Chelsea.

Joe was a regular in the QoS side for several years, until his place was taken by the 1938 arrival of the mercurial Tommy Lang, who had been the star of Newcastle United's 1932 FA Cup-winning side.

Joe drifted out of the side but his time in Scotland is recalled by one of the all-time great newspaper headlines. After Joe had scored Queens' goal in a 1-0 victory at Celtic Park, the Glasgow evening billboards ran with: "Tulip Tiptoes Through The Shamrocks".

■ *This is an example of a damaged archive photo. At some point in the past, a sports editor has called for a head-and-shoulders pic of Jimmy Anderson, and the re-touching artists have painted around him (to give the impression that he is standing alone), sketched in some extra shirt sleeve, and the rest of the players would have been cropped off. This was all to the detriment of Willie Anderson, whose face has been covered. I apologise to Willie for this abuse. This was, of course, years before the era of the digital image, but is an example of the working lives these photos have had.*

■ **Back row, from left: Jimmy Anderson, Willie Savage, Willie Fotheringham, Willie Culbert, Gordon, Adam Allan. Front: Willie Anderson, Laurie Cumming, Nesbitt, McGinley, Joe Tulip.**

1934~Wee Rovers become champions

ONLY an Albion Rovers supporter could judge whether reaching the Scottish Cup Final in 1920, or winning the Division Two title in 1933-34 is the club's greatest ever achievement.

This photo shows that championship side of 1934. The club played in blue at that time, the current yellow and red colours were adopted in the 1960s.

The thirties was a good decade for the Wee Rovers. Two years later, a cup tie with Rangers would draw Cliftonhill's biggest ever crowd, 27,381, and promotion would be won again (a second-place finish) in 1937-38.

The war came at just the wrong time for a club that had spent four of the previous five seasons in the top division.

When competitive football was re-established for 1946-47, Rovers were placed in Division B (despite having been in the top division when hostilities started).

Since then they have spent just one further season, 1948-49, in Scottish football's top flight.

■ **Another damaged photo. Rovers 1933-34. Back, from left: William Bruce, Donnelly (partially obscured), Andrew Waddell, Crosskey, Beath, John McPhee, Browning. Front: Kirk, J. Beath, Liddell, Barclay.**

1934~Denied Matt's talents

O N only three occasions in this book, we will look at teams from south of the Border (see also pages 46 and 174). The reasons will be obvious.

Matt Busby played for Denny Hibs in Lanarkshire while working down the pit, but signed for Manchester City at the age of 18 in 1928. He played more than 200 times for The Sky Blues, winning the FA Cup in 1934. He was transferred to Liverpool for £8,000, in 1936 and formed, with fellow Scots Jimmy McDougall and Tom (Tiny) Bradshaw, what is often regarded as Anfield's best ever half-back line.

And, as everyone knows, he became the trophy-laden Manchester United manager, 1945-69 and 1970-71.

Matt guested for Hibs during the war, but the Scottish game never saw his managerial talents.

■ **Manchester City 1934. Back, from left: Wilf Wild (manager), Matt Busby, Laurie Barnett, Frank Swift, Bill Dale, Jimmy McLuckie, Jackie Bray, Sandy Bell (trainer). Front: Ernie Toseland, Bobby Marshall, Sam Cowan, Fred Tilson, Alec Herd, Eric Brook.**

1935~All-time high scorer

THE greatest Scottish goalscorer of all-time is Celtic's Jimmy McGrory. He scored 472 goals in 445 league and cup games

He was five foot, six inches, with shoulders like a Titan, and so good at diving headers that he was nicknamed "The Human Torpedo".

His record will never be surpassed.

■ **Celtic 1933. Back, from left: Bertie Thomson, M. Kennedy, George Paterson, John Divers, John Connor. Middle: Willie Dunn, Jock Wallace, M. McDonald, John Boyle, Joe Kennaway, John Morrison, Peter McGonagle, Hughie Smith, Willie Buchan, Frank O'Donnell, Jack Quskay (trainer), Alec Thomson. Front: Peter Wilson, John Crum, Jimmy McGrory, Danny Dawson, Jimmy McStay (captain), Willie Hughes, Bobby Hogg, Hugh O'Donnell, Charlie Napier.**

1935~The thud of a wet, heavy ball

FOOTBALLS of yesteryear, indeed, until the 1970s, were leather tubs stitched round an innertube. When it rained, the leather stretched, and water soaked in. The ball became a heavy, soggy lump. This made the game very different.

To make matters worse, the science of pitch drainage was in its infancy. On wet days, surfaces quickly became gluey quagmires.

Saturday April 20, 1935, was a day of heavy rain across Scotland, leading to some games being abandoned. But the Rangers v Hamilton Academical Scottish Cup Final went ahead at Hampden (in those days league games were played the same day as cup finals).

The final was one of those games in which players finished the 90 minutes caked in mud from head to toe. The athleticism and strength of Rangers men like Torry Gillick, Jimmy Simpson and Bob McPhail coped better in the glaur and Rangers won 2-1.

It was the second, and so far last, time The Accies had been to a Scottish Cup Final.

■ **Hamilton Academical, cup finalists of 1935. Back, from left: Jamie Thomson, John Bulloch, Jimmy McStay, Jim Morgan, Johnny Cox, John Dewar. Front: Bobby Reid, Bertie Harrison, Dave Wilson, Willie McLaren, Jimmy King.**

1937~What might they have achieved?

BILL SHANKLY is the subject of the second of our visits south of the Border. Shankly was born in Glenbuck, Ayrshire, one of 10 children, five boys and five girls. All of the brothers played professional football.

Shankly signed for Carlisle in 1932 after losing his job as a miner. The gritty half-back was transferred to Preston North End for £500 the following season and played there until 1949.

He is famed, though, as manager of Liverpool 1959-74. Shankly built a legend on Merseyside. His name has become a definition of a way to play the game we call football.

It is a tragedy that the managerial talents of men such as Bill Shankly and Matt Busby were lost to the Scottish game. What might they have achieved in their homeland?

Imagine Shankly as boss of Hearts or Rangers, or Busby in charge of Hibs or Aberdeen. What trophies, home and abroad, would they have won?

■ **Preston North End 1937-38. Back, from left: Andy Beattie, Frank O'Donnell, Henry Holdcroft, George Lowrie, Mick Burns, Jimmy Milne, Jimmy Dougall. Middle: Hugh O'Donnell, Bud Maxwell, Billy Tremelling, Will Scott (trainer), John Jennings, Len Gallimore, Bill Shankly. Front: Willie Fagan, Joe Beresford.**

1938~Strange and romantic cup exploits of East Fife

IT rarely happens in the modern game. East Fife were a Second Division club in the 1937-38 season, but they won the Scottish Cup. They remained the only team from the second tier to do so until Hibs matched the feat a full 78 years later.

The Fifers didn't even do particularly well in Division Two that '37-38 season, finishing sixth behind champions Raith Rovers. But then their opponents in the final, Kilmarnock, only avoided relegation by a single point, conceding 91 goals in their 38 league games.

The first final was a 1-1 draw, in front of 80,091 at Hampden.

To modern readers, perhaps even more remarkable than a lower league club winning the cup would be the inclusion in their replay line-up of another club's player.

East Fife's left-half, Andy Herd, was injured in the first final, but the men of Methil were able to make John Harvey, of Hearts, an "emergency signing".

Harvey, who would go on to manage Hearts in the 1960s, came in, played one game only for East Fife, and left again — clutching a Scottish Cup medal.

That replay drew a remarkable midweek crowd of 92,716 to Hampden. Levenmouth was completely deserted that evening.

The score was 2-2 at the end of the 90 minutes, but a Larry Millar strike and a Dan McKerell header, both in the second half of extra time, sent the cup to Fife for the first time — indeed the furthest north it had yet travelled in its 60-year history.

■ The cup finals 12. Back, from left: Davie Russell, Willie Laird, Bobby Tait, Jimmy Milton, John Harvey, loaned-in Andy Herd. Front: Tommy Adams, Larry Millar, Bobby McCartney, John Sneddon, Eddie McLeod, Danny McKerrell.

1939~The war years

THE Second World War stopped football in its tracks. The 1939-40 season was abandoned after five games had been played in the Scottish First Division and four in the Second.

"Emergency leagues" were set up, but only after the express permission of Home Secretary Sir John Anderson was obtained. Scottish Eastern and Western divisions of 16 teams were established. But with "guests" taking a game for whichever club they were stationed close to, the leagues were never truly competitive

Football didn't properly get under way again until the 1946-47 season — but some clubs suffered more than others due to the long break.

Cowdenbeath had been out of the top league for five years, but won the 1938-39 Second Division.

However, after the seven-year hiatus they weren't reinstated to the First Division, but instead were placed in Division Two. Apart from 1970-71, they haven't competed in the top league since.

This photo was taken in August 1939, with the optimisim of a new top-flight season shining on every player's face. Charmingly, the referee was invited in to the photo too.

■ **Cowdenbeath's full muster of 23 signed men for 1939-40. Back, from left: James McColl, R. Moodie, J. Devlin, F. Harper, A. McLean, P. Playfair, I. McDowall, W. Knox. Middle: W. Clark, R. McLellan, P. Gillespie (referee), W. Gillies, G. Jordan, J. Hill, R. Rougvie, A. Rhodie, J. Littlejohn. Front: J. Watters, A. Milne, G. Wilson, W. Reid, R. Boag, W. Hillan, K. Stewart, unknown.**

1947~10-0 wins, in two games running

WINNING 10-0 is rare. Winning 10-0 in two games in a row is unheard of. Yet that's what Dundee did on March 8, 1947, away to Alloa, and then March 22 at home to Dunfermline. It is a record unmatched in Scotland, probably the world.

Top scorer in these games was powerful, fleet-footed centre-forward Bert Juliussen, who grabbed six in the first game then seven in the next. Can you name another player who has scored 13 goals in two games?

Despite winning the last of the wartime B Divisions in 1945-46, Dundee had been placed in Division B again in '46-47. This was for ease of travel, rather than the quality of the team. In truth Dundee were far stronger than the teams around them.

The Dark Blues won the league at a canter, scoring 113 goals in 26 games, conceding only 30 and losing just twice. They put Celtic out of the Scottish Cup but lost to eventual winners Aberdeen in the quarter-final.

■ **Dundee 1947. Back, from left: Reuben Bennett, John Laurie, R. Wilson, George Stewart, John Lynch, A. Smith, J. McAlpine, Peter Rattray, P. Barrie. Middle: W. Cameron, Bob Bowman, Doug Cowie, Gibby McKenzie, Andy Irvine, Bobby Ancell, J. Dickson, Tommy Gray, Jack Bruce, Alfie Boyd, Andy McCall. Front: Alex Stott, Ally Gunn, Ernie Ewen, Ronnie Turnbull, George Anderson, Bert Juliussen, Reggie Smith, John Patillo, George Hill.**

1947~East Fife win League Cup

AS with their Scottish Cup win of 1938, East Fife were the first club to win the League Cup while not playing in Scotland's top flight (the only club to do so since are Raith Rovers in 1994-95).

The Methil men, mind you, raced to the Scottish League Division B title of 1947-48, finishing 11 points ahead of Albion Rovers and scoring 103 goals while doing so.

One of the main reasons for the team's potency was the inclusion of the gifted Tommy Adams at inside-right.

A newspaper report of that 1947-48 League Cup Final replay 4-1 win over Falkirk starts off: "A rollicking hat-trick by Davie Duncan. A half-back line who were a whole team in themselves.

And little Tommy Adams, whose every kick showed more guile than any half-dozen other moves."

Born in Glasgow in 1916, Tommy was one of East Fife's greatest ever players. In a career interrupted by the second world war he played 248 competitive games for the Methil Men between 1935 and 1949, scoring 78 goals.

But games and goals statistics never tell the full story.

Tommy was a wizard with a football, able to thread passes through the tightest of defences, turn on the proverbial sixpence and ghost past even the great defenders of the day.

He was a much-loved figure with the crowds at Bayview and his guileful, inspiring performance in that 1947 League

Cup Final is the stuff of legend in the Kingdom of Fife.

Sadly, like too many genius players over the years, he was inexplicably never recognised with a Scottish international cap. It has long been the belief among the supporters of provincial clubs that their stars are overlooked

Tommy would walk (with a feint left, then switch to the right) into today's national team...but then he'd have been snapped up by Chelsea, Barcelona or Juventus in the modern era.

■ **Chaired by team mates Morris, Stewart and Philp, Tommy Adams, East Fife F.C. captain, proudly clutches the trophy after that League Cup Final replay victory over Falkirk at Hampden.**

1948~Young Jock

EVERYONE starts somewhere. No one could know that the strapping young man in the back row of this 1948 promotion-winning Albion Rovers team group would go on to become one of the greatest figures in Scottish football history — not even Jock himself (he is 26 in this photo).

Jock had been a miner through the war years, which was a reserved occupation — he had to go down the pit, like it or not.

But in his sparc time Jock played for Junior outfit Blantyre Vics. He was asked along to The Wee Rovers in 1942 and played his first game as a trialist in a 4-4 draw with Celtic.

A few weeks later he signed as a part-timer and would feature in nearly 100 games for the Coatbridge club. His highlight at Cliftonhill was promotion with this line-up in season 1947-48, although the club would spend just a single season in the Scottish League Division A, as it was at the time.

Non-league Welsh outfit Llanelli Town offered him a full-time contract in 1950, at a princely £12 a week and Jock moved to Wales.

But in 1951 Celtic paid £1200 to bring him back to Glasgow, setting in motion a chain of events that would lead to great things.

■ **Albion Rovers 1948. Back row, from left: Alex Muir, Davie Martin, Joe Henderson, Jock Stein, Robert Beath, Jim Hunter. Front: John Craig, Neil MacKinnon, Arthur Carrie, John Love, Doug Wallace.**

1950~The Qualifying Cup

THE Scottish Qualifying Cup, 1895 to 2007, was one of the great Scottish football institutions — although tucked away from the sight of the big clubs.

It was established to allow teams from the Highland, South and, East of Scotland Leagues to progress to the Scottish Cup proper. The idea was to cut out badly mis-matched ties in the early rounds.

Until 1930-31 it was a national competition, but split into North-South regions. After 1931, all the semi-finalists qualified for the Scottish Cup proper. Regularly, one of these qualifiers would win through to the Third Round, when the big guns entered, and many a "League" club fell to a giantkilling act by one of these qualifiers.

The competition was scrapped for the 2007-08 season, when the Scottish Cup preliminary rounds were extended to take in all clubs affiliated to the SFA.

■ **Brechin City won the Qualifying Cup (left) in 1950. Right: their team which went on to play Celtic in the Scottish Cup proper that season. Back from left: Archie Paterson, Atkinson, Shaw, Bennett, Smith, Mitchell. Front: Fraser, Robbie, Davie Paris, Hind, Henderson.**

■ Clyde's Division B champions 1952. Back, from left: Directors Dr John Dunn, J. Riddell, J. MacMahon, J. Taylor, Phil Bauld, Frank Mennie, Jim Campbell, Bob Milligan, Don Cornock, J. Scoullier (director), W.P. Dunn (chairman), Owen McCabe (director). Middle: C. Miller (asst. trainer), Willie Barclay, Basil Keogh, Sam Dunn, Jack Lindsay, Bobby Sommerville, Willie Miller, Charlie Thomson, Willie Wilson, Billy McPhail, Sammy Baird, John Clifford, Jack Henderson, T. Colquhoun (director). Front: J. Wilkie (asst. trainer), John Haddow (trainer), H. Friel, George Bolton, Duncan Smith, Tommy Ring, Harry Haddock, Hugh Long, Tommy Anderson, John Buchanan, Peter Galletly, J. Robb, Archie Robertson, Paddy Travers (manager), A. McCormack (asst. trainer). Trophies: Division B League, Glasgow Cup, Glasgow Merchants Charity Cup, B Division Supplementary Cup.

1952~Dundee's Steel team

HE was a superstar, a giant of the game when he signed for Dundee. Billy Steel set a British transfer record (£15,500) when he moved from Morton to Derby County in 1947, and a Scottish transfer fee record (£22,500) when Dundee brought him back north of the Border in 1950.

And he was worth every penny. Dundee's crowds immediately went up — 34,000 were at his debut v. Aberdeen at Dens Park on September 23, 1950.

The Dees, inspired by their Steel capture, beat Rangers 3-2 in the 1951 League Cup Final. They lost the 1952 Scottish Cup Final, to Motherwell (see next page) but would become the first club to retain the League Cup by beating Kilmarnock in '52.

But if Billy was the headliner, he certainly wasn't this 1950s Dundee team's only remarkable player. They had Bobby Flavell at centre-forward, who caused a sensation in 1950 by leaving Hearts to sign for Colombian side Millonarios, where he played alongside the great Alfredo di Stefano.

The Colombian league was in dispute with FIFA, so refused to pay transfer fees and attracted stars from all over Europe and South America. Attendances boomed for a three-year period. Bobby played a season there but was suspended and heavily fined on his return to Scotland.

Inside-forward Bert Henderson would later manage Arbroath FC for an astonishing 18 years.

Tommy Gallacher, the son of Celtic legend Patsy Gallacher, would become a respected football journalist and spent nearly 30 years as The Courier's chief football writer in Dundee.

Goalkeeper Bill Brown would become a Spurs legend as part of their double-winning team of 1961 and the first British side to win a European trophy, the Cup Winners' Cup, two years later.

■ **Dundee FC 1952. Back, from left: Tommy Gallagher, Gerry Follon, Bill Brown, Doug Cowie, Jack Cowan. Middle: Johnny Pattillo, four un-named directors, trainer Reggie Smith. Front: Jimmy Toner, Bobby Flavell, another un-named director, Alf Boyd, George Anderson (manager), Billy Steel, George Christie.**

1952~Was it Well's best performance?

IT is probably impossible to definitively identify a club's best ever performance, but a 4-0 Scottish Cup Final win, in front of a crowd of 136,990, would have to be a candidate. There were around 5,000 more locked out of Hampden, with several arrests as disappointed and angry fans tried to force their way in.

Motherwell would win the cup again nearly 40 years later in 1991. But while the '91 final was a great game, the boys of '52 put on a show of total domination over Dundee. It was 0-0 at half-time, at a rainy Hampden, but 'Well were unstoppable in the second half — "Never in its long history has the trophy been more worthily won", said the next day's Sunday Post.

Manager was George Stevenson, who had been an integral part of The Steelmen's league championship side of 1932. He'd led 'Well to the League Cup in 1950, and runners-up to Celtic in the 1951 Scottish Cup. But April 19, 1952, was his great managerial triumph.

■ **Motherwell, April 1951: Back, from left: Willie Kilmarnock, Donald McLeod, Dick Hamilton, Andrew Paton, Willie Redpath, Archie Shaw. Front: Willie Watters, James Forrest, Archie Kelly, Jimmy Watson, Johnny Aitkenhead.**

1952~High boots and shinpads

FOOTBALL boots started to change in the 1960s — and haven't stopped changing since. But before then the style remained constant for decades.

Boots were ankle-high, made of thick leather and designed for foot protection rather than ball control. In the rain they absorbed moisture and doubled in weight.

Leather studs, or sometimes bars, were nailed to the thick leather soles. Screw-in studs weren't invented until the 1950s, in Germany, and took several years to become widely-used.

Laces were long and almost universally were looped round the sole before being tied.

Similarly, old-fashioned shinpads were leather or canvas, often with bamboo sticks inserted into slim, vertical pockets to offer maximum protection. These, too, underwent little change for many years. These heavy pads might also have robust ankle guards and would be very long, covering the wearer from knee to foot.

This gave footballers, as can be seen in the photo on the right, that distinctive thick-legged, almost armour-plated look.

Socks were heavy, woolly and very long, and could be folded down in a variety of ways.

■ Forfar Athletic, 1952. Back, from left: Eric Harper, James McCluskey, Adam Good, John McNellis, Derek McKenzie, Edward Falconer. Front: Fred Downs, Stewart McLean, William Brown, Colin McLean, James Robertson.

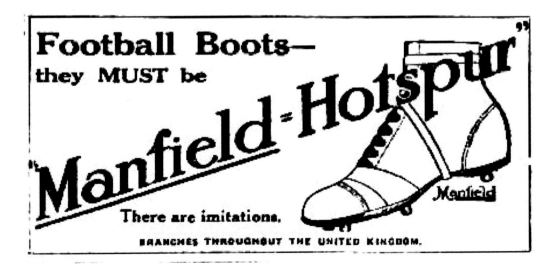

Football Boots—
they MUST be

"Manfield Hotspur"

There are imitations.

Manfield

BRANCHES THROUGHOUT THE UNITED KINGDOM.

CHRISTIE—HE GOT THE WINNER

FLEMING— GOAL 2

GARDINER —GOAL 1

■ Celebrations in 1953 after East Fife won the League Cup. The goalscorer headlines were added by a 1950s artist.

■ Celebrations in 1954 outside Hampden after Celtic had won the Scottish Cup.

■ Rangers 1954. Back, from left: Andrew Simpson, Jim Rodger, William McRae, Gordon McKenzie, Willie Woodburn, George Niven, John Neil, Bobby Brown, R. Carmichael, Colin Liddell, Ross Menzies, John Woods, Ian Wellands. Middle: Scott Symon (manager), William Simpson, Alan Elliot, Willie Waddell, Jim Pryde, Ian McColl, Duncan Stanners, John Prentice, William McCulloch, William Paton, Eric Caldow, John Hubbard, Joe Craven (assist. trainer). Front: Hamish McMillan, Derek Grierson, Hunter MacMillan, Sammy Cox, D. McIntosh, George London, George McKenzie, John Little, William Gardiner, William Findlay, Ralph Brand, Jim Smith (trainer).

1954~Ibrox Iron Curtain

THE famous Rangers defensive line-up of the late 1940s and early '50s was known as The Iron Curtain. Indeed, many football fans in Scotland thought the term "Iron Curtain" referred only to the highly efficient Ibrox back line, not anything to do with some European political divide.

The most recognised defence was Bobby Brown in goal, full-backs George Young and Jock "Tiger" Shaw, and half-backs Willie Woodburn, Ian McColl and Sammy Cox. Their names are still spoken of in tones of respect.

In a high-scoring era, Rangers' goals-against column in 1949-50, for instance, was 26 conceded in 30 league games.

■ **Right: Tiger Shaw, on the shoulders of Sammy Cox and Willie Thornton, with the 1950 Scottish Cup.**

1955~Dave's Dons

LIKE Hughie Gallacher, Dave Halliday's incredible goalscoring feats aren't as celebrated as they should be because they took place before the war.

Dumfries-born Halliday started his career at QoS and St Mirren, before moving to Dundee where he scored 38 goals in the 38 games of the 1923-24 season. A £4,000 fee took him to Sunderland. He is still in the record books for scoring 100 English top-division goals in the shortest time (101 games). He is also the only man to score more than 35 league goals in four successive seasons in England's top division. He then played for Arsenal and Manchester City before applying for the Aberdeen manager's job in 1937.

The Dons had always been a big club, but had never won national silverware. Halliday won every available domestic honour in his 15 years at Pittodrie.

But this photo of Halliday's 1954-55 League Champions has another figure whose story is quite incredible. Harry Yorston played 277 games for Aberdeen and scored 141 goals. But that's not what he is remembered for. See page 80.

■ **Aberdeen FC 1954-55. Back, from left: George Kelly, Jack Dunbar, Reg Morrison, Fred Martin, Ian MacFarlane. Third row: Crawford Clelland, Joe O'Neil, Jim Clunie, Hugh Hay, Teddy Scott, Ian McNeill. Second row: D. Shaw (trainer), Jimmy Ingram, Bobby Wilson, Archie Glen, Billy Smith, Ivor Smith, John Brown, Bob Wishart, Jack Allister, Jimmy Wallace, B. Alexander (assist. trainer). Front: John Allan, Norman Davidson, Jimmy Brown, Bobby Paterson, Paddy Buckley, Dave Halliday (manager), Jimmy Mitchell, Alec Young, Harry Yorston, George Hamilton, George Mulhall.**

1956~Daft team shirt design is nothing new

IN the modern game, a club's kit-manufacturer dresses the team in a fancy new get-up every season. The idea is to sell replica shirts to long-suffering fans. Sometimes the design, and the shade of the traditional club colours, is quite imaginative. Or, to use another word, ridiculous.

You have to wonder what the players think each new season when they are presented with the haute couture creations of the fashion designers.

This didn't happen in the rough, tough, olden days when men were men, shinpads were thick, and club doctors were nervous.

Or did it?

St Johnstone's 1956 departure from cotton jerseys raised an eyebrow or two.

Newspapers of the time described The Saintees' shirts as "natty, new, nylon, and blue". They were very shiny and must have stood out quite brightly against the dreich skies of a Perth November.

The shouted opinions of opposition supporters, and players, are probably best not repeated.

■ **St Johnstone 1956. Back, from left: Jimmy Woodcock, Ian Palmer, Andy Bell, Ernie Ewen, Ally Rae, Alex Menzies. Front: Gordon Fraser, Peter Rattray, Ian Rodger, George Whitelaw, Ian Samson.**

■ **Celtic 1956. Back, from left: Craig, Meechan, Jack, Bonnar, Evans, Haughney, Fallon. Middle: W. Johnstone (trainer), Goldie, Boden, Walsh, McCreadie, Auld, McKay, McAlinden, J. McGrory (manager), J. Gribben (assistant trainer). Front: Ryan, Collins, Peacock, McPhail, Tully, Mochan.**

■ **Kilmarnock 1957. Back, from left: Ralph Collins, Jim Stewart, Jimmy Brown, Rab Stewart, Willie Toner, George Taggart. Front: Billy Muir, Willie Harvey, Gerry Mays, Bertie Black, David Burns.**

1957~Harold Davis, a warrior of the game

HAROLD DAVIS fought in the Korean War and was badly wounded by machine-gun fire. He spent two years in hospital with abdominal and foot injuries.

That he lived, is remarkable. That he carved out a career as a top-class footballer is amazing.

His against-the-odds survival left Harold determined to make the utmost of the rest of his life, be peerlessly fit and to conquer any challenge. This never-say-die attitude and his natural athleticism made Davis a formidable footballer.

He played eight seasons for Rangers, winning seven trophies and a runners-up medal in the 1961 European Cup Winners' Cup.

■ Rangers 1957. Back, from left: W. Smith, J. Miller, I. Atkinson, W. Logie, C. Wright, G. Niven, W. Ritchie, J. Valentine, H. Neill, Harold Davis, A. Austin. Middle: M. Murray, J. Currie, W. Simpson, W. Stevenson, R. Morrison, J. Walker, S. Baird, W. Moles, D. Kichenbrand, G. Thomson, J. Little, J. Queen, J. Craven (assistant trainer). Front: Mr J. S. Symon (manager), E. Caldow, G. Duncan, A. Scott, T. Robertson, I. McColl (captain), S. McCorquodale, J. Hubbard, R. Brand, R. Shearer, H. Melrose, D. Wilson, D. Kinnear (trainer).

1957~Fish is better

HARRY YORSTON was the nephew of another Dons great, Benny Yorston, who still holds the record for highest number of goals (38) in a single season (1929-30).

Harry was also a prolific striker, although he had a sometimes difficult relationship with his club's fans. He said, "As the local boy in the team, I used to get barracked if I put a foot wrong. There were times I'd get abuse just walking down Union Street."

He won a Scotland cap in 1954 and contributed an invaluable 12 league goals as Aberdeen took the 1954-55 title.

But at the end of the 1956-57 season, aged 28 and at the height of his goalscoring powers, Harry sensationally announced he was quitting professional football to take up what he described as a more lucrative job as a porter at Aberdeen fish market. He told reporters he'd earn 10 shillings a week more at the docks.

It was a story that rocked Scottish football, but Harry had no regrets. When interviewed in 1986 he said, "You had to start the job before you were 30. To me, it was perfectly logical."

He continued to play football, though — for the Fish Market Porters amateur team.

But in 1972 Harry, annoyed at his lack of success when playing the football pools, for a change got his wife Johan to fill in his coupon. She chose birth dates, house numbers and anniversaries — and they won £170,000, around £1.6 million today (though initial reports, see right, put it at just £100,000).

Harry gave up the fish market after the windfall, the 3am starts not being his favourite thing. But he grew bored and became a driver, working for a hairdressers, then a print firm in Aberdeen.

He returned to Pittodrie in the mid-1970s to help revamp the club's youth policy. Players such as Neale Cooper and John Hewitt were recruited. But Harry walked away from the club again, citing a lack of interest in the youths from manager Ally McLeod.

Harry went on to become a Scottish scout for Manchester United for a few years.

Despite his fame and fortune, Harry remained a proudly "ordinary bloke" for the rest of his days, a tee-totaller with no pretentions to a jet-setting life. He was in no hurry to move from his comfortable house in the Aberdeen suburb of Craigiebuckler.

Sadly, Harry passed away in 1992, aged 62, after suffering a brain tumour.

Harry Yorston nets a first dividend

FORMER DON WINS £100,000

That's my winning line . . . a happy Harry Yorston, his fortune-winning coupon copy aloft, gets a hug from his wife Johan on hearing the wonderful news today

FORMER Dons' star "Golden Boy" Harry Yorston has won at least £100,000 on the pools. And the final figure may be as high as £150,000.

Cliff fall boy 'critical'

A BUCKSBURN schoolboy who slipped and fell 60 feet onto rocks in one of two separate cliff accidents on the North-east coast, was critical today at Aberdeen Royal Infirmary, Foresterhill.

And RAF serviceman Anthony Nurmi (25) injured when he fell from cliffs near his station at RAF Buchan, was said to be "quite comfortable".

Schoolboy Frank Andrew, 1 Hopetoun Terrace, was walking with his brother Neil (20), and a friend along a rough cliff path at Winnyfold, near Cruden Bay, when he lost his footing and plunged into a gully, known locally as "Hell's Hole".

Cruden Bay coastguards were alerted and three of them descended the gully, strapped the injured youth to a stretcher and hauled him up.

In the second accident LAC Nurmi fell from the cliffs after the rock face collapsed beneath him.

It is understood he was rescued by members of RAF Buchan's expedition and training team.

The 42-year-old former Scots international and his family will fly to Glasgow tomorrow to be presented with their cheque from Littlewoods.

Today an anxious Harry, who is immediately giving up his fish market porter's job, sat by the telephone in his semi-detached home at 42 Burnieboozle Crescent, Aberdeen, awaiting confirmation of his win.

It was Harry's attractive wife Johan, a nurse at Aberdeen Royal Infirmary, Foresterhill, who filled in the winning coupon.

Out of a total of eight scoring draws and 12 non-scoring draws on Saturday, she picked six scoring draws and two non-scoring draws on a five bob Lit-plan.

A Littlewoods representative called on the lucky couple last night to tell them they had won at least £100,000 — and possibly much more.

Said Harry: "We were expecting £20,000 or £30,000 anyway but he said it would be six figures.

"He phoned first from the station and asked for me. I was out playing football with my son, Harry (7) and my wife answered the phone. She asked who was speaking and he said: 'If I say I'm from Littlewoods you will understand.'

"He said to leave me playing football and he would come up to the house. He was to be contacting Liverpool today in case of a late claim, but it seems unlikely now.

"At present I'm one of

three winners sharing in the region of £400,000-£500,000."

This morning Lady Luck herself, Mrs Yorston, was being treated to an expensive hairdo at one of Aberdeen's leading hairdressing salons by her still unbelieving husband.

He told the "Evening Express" he had been trying the pools for years without winning a penny, and only three months ago decided to let Johan pick the numbers.

With predictable feminine intuition she latched on to family birthdays, and addresses—with devastating success.

Life, say the Yorstons, will go on much the same as before. For them there will be no big house, no Rolls Royce in the drive, and no round the world cruises.

Aberdeen's biggest ever individual pools winner grinned: "This isn't going to affect our way of life at all. It's just one of those things. A lot of people are going to get the good of it—particularly our son."

For Harry, a tee-totaller who enjoys the quiet life, countries like Italy and Spain hold no attractions.

His idea of a celebration holiday is a few weeks "somewhere in this country" with young Harry after the schools break up for the summer in June.

FORTUNE

And Johan, who works weekends at the hospital, and has just applied for a district nursing post, is going to carry

Rail situ 'Not so di

AS SCOTLAND faced Day Three of the rail travellers unexpectedly found they had to con disruptions.

There was a dramatic improvement on yesterday near chaotic scenes hundreds of passengers left stranded, or hours behind schedule.

Although British Rail to run any direct service from Aberdeen to Glasgow the morning, most passengers managed to reach their west via Edinburgh.

Inverness - bound trains were less lucky, with management forced to the line between 10.4

Labour challenge to Tories

1957~A day that Celtic fans still sing about

THERE'S nothing quite like beating your fiercest rivals. But putting seven past them in a cup final is quite another matter. Celtic's 7-1 defeat of Rangers in the 1957 League Cup final remains a British record for a cup final. The Celtic supporters still sing of it.

This was a day that saw one of the great team performances in Scottish football history. As The Sunday Post said the day after the final: "Rangers hadn't one really good player. Celtic hadn't a bad one. Not even an ordinary one."

However, in truth, football isn't as simple as that. A team needs a leader, and that leader has to provide inspiration. The Celtic team of the 1950s had Bobby Evans. In what was, overall, a fallow period for trophies, Evans was a shining light. A man who drove his team on, who led by example, and who spread his personal will-to-win throughout his team.

Bobby Evans' name is sparsely mentioned in reports of that 7-1 final, but the victory was built upon him.

■ **Celtic 1956-57. Back, from left: Duncan McKay, Bobby Evans, John Divers, John Bonnar, Eric Smith, Bertie Auld, Sammy Wilson. Middle: W. Johnstone (trainer), Frank Meechan, Ian White, Sean Fallon, John Jack, Vince Ryan, Jim Sharkey, John Colrain, J. Gribben (asst. trainer), Jimmy McGrory (manager). Front: John Higgins, Bobby Collins, Billy McPhail, Willie Fernie, Bertie Peacock, Charlie Tully, Neil Mochan.**

1958~Hearts of goals

THE most potent attacking line-up Scottish football has ever seen was the Hearts team that won the league in 1957-58.

The side scored the most goals ever seen in a top-flight season (132 in 34 games) and are the only team in Scottish football's highest division to record a goal-difference of better than 100. They let in just 29 goals. League places were reckoned by goal average in those days, of course.

They scored a further 26 goals in the Scottish and League Cups.

They lost one league game, 2-1 away to Clyde on November 23, and finished 13 points clear of Rangers. The title was clinched with a 3-2 victory over St Mirren at Love Street on April 12, 1958.

Manager, Tommy Walker, has been described as Hearts' most influential figure of all time. He played 14 seasons for the club and managed them for 15 years. Tommy built his '57-58 side paying a transfer fee for only one man, Bobby Kirk from Raith Rovers.

■ **Hearts 1958. Back, from left: Alfie Conn, Bobby Blackwood, John Lough, George Glover, Wilson Brown, George Robertson, Gordon Marshall, Willie Bauld, Billy Higgins, Jimmy Wardhaugh, Tom MacKenzie. Middle: D. McLeod (asst. manager), Andy Bowman, Jim McFadzean, John Cumming, Peter Smith, George Thomson, John McIntosh, Bobby Kirk, Billy Lindores, John Harvey (trainer). Front: Hugh Goldie, Johnny Hamilton, Andy Fraser, Dave Mackay, Ian Crawford, Jimmy Murray, Danny Paton.**

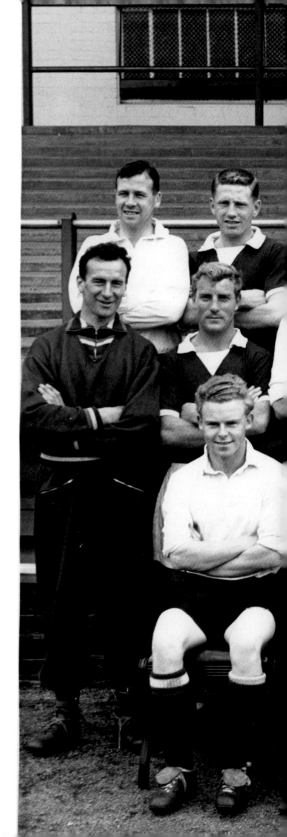

1958~Why a moment sticks in the memory

IT is a "truth" of football that there is often a definitive "one thing" a player will stick in the memory for. It could be a goal, a nutmeg, a trophy win, even a sending-off or a mistake. But whenever that player is mentioned, the "one thing" springs to mind.

Slim Jim Baxter performed three keepie-ups on the left wing as Scotland beat England 3-2 at Wembley in 1967.

Baxter had scored both Scotland's goals in the 2-1 win over England at Wembley 1963, but that is often forgotten. He is remembered for a gallus few seconds of showboating more than any of his other great games and goals.

It deserves to be remembered. There were six minutes left in the 1967 game, England were world champions, Scotland were winning 2-0, Denis Law

and Jim McCalliog had just performed back-heeled passes. Then Jim did it.

Baxter's keepie-ups are often described as a distillation of what our brand of football, the glory game, is all about. It will be talked of as long as fitbas are kicked in Scotland.

Jim was a Sunderland player at the time of those Wembley exploits and is known as a Rangers legend, but began his career in Kirkcaldy under revered Raith Rovers manager Bert Herdman.

■ **Raith Rovers 1958. Back, from left: Willie Polland, John Lockerbie, Jim Thorburn, Andy Leigh, Willie McNaught, Jim Baxter. Front: Jimmy McEwan, John Ward, George Dobbie, Jackie Williamson, Johnny Urquhart.**

1959~The genius and tragedy of John White

IF you can impress your team-mates, you're doing well. John White made a big impression on his Scotland team-mate Dave Mackay, scoring in the first minute of his debut in a famous 3-2 win for Scotland over West Germany on May 6, 1959.

Mackay went back to Tottenham, who he had just signed for, and told his new boss Bill Nicholson about this skinny laddie from a Falkirk side that had just been relegated.

Spurs were worried that the frail-looking White wouldn't stand up to the rigours of football south of the Border, so Nicholson contacted the army to ask what the Musselburgh boy's fitness had been like during National Service. Upon learning he'd been a cross-country champion, the London club splashed out £22,000 — to all but complete the team that would mark up English football's first "double" of the 20th Century.

John died, aged just 27, in 1964 as a result of a lightning strike on Crews Hill golf course on the northern outskirts of London.

John's nickname was "the ghost" because he would ghost into space on a football field. His spirit lives on at Alloa and Falkirk, his Scottish clubs, as well as at Tottenham Hotspur.

■ **Falkirk 1959: Back, from left: Jimmy McIntosh, Billy Price, Tommy Younger, Bill McCarry, Jim Richmond, Ian Rae. Front: Jim Oliver, John White, John Hunter, Tom Moran, Robertson.**

1959~Ayr United's Price of success

TO Ayr United fans, the years from 1955 to 1962 are known as "The Price Era". The name is given in honour of Peter Price.

The Honest Men won the Second Division in fine style in 1958-59, finishing nine points ahead of Arbroath.

Their centre-forward, Ayr-born Peter Price, scored an incredible 37 goals in the 35 league games he played, and 51 goals in total that season.

The next year in the First Division was one of the best in Ayr's history to that point. The club finished eighth, a place above Celtic, and recorded away victories at Ibrox and Celtic Park.

Peter was an all-round footballer as well as a superb finisher. He provided assists, was involved in build-up play, and was a mesmerising dribbler.

He scored 27 goals in season 1959-60 in Division 1 and is, to this day, Ayr's all-time top scorer with 213 competitive goals.

■ **Back, from left: William Gilmour (assistant trainer), Bobby Thomson, John Telfer, Ian Hamilton, Willie McIntyre, Jim McLean, Alex Glen, Mr Matt Pollock (chairman). Front: Eddie Summers (trainer), Alastair McIntyre, Sam McMillan, Peter Price, Willie Paton, Jim McGhee, Jacky Cox (manager).**

1960~How could the Hi-Hi die?

THIS 1960-61 Third Lanark team was one of the best in the club's history. They finished third in the First Division behind Rangers and Kilmarnock, scoring 100 goals in the process.

It was the bones of the team that had narrowly lost the 1959 League Cup Final to Hearts, 2-1.

In the 1962 close season they would sell top scorer (he'd grabbed 42 goals) Alex Harley to Manchester City for £19,500 (just short of half a million adjusted to today's prices).

But within six years the club had disappeared.

The 1965-66 season was disastrous. Only three league wins inevitably brought relegation. On Saturday, April 15, 1967, Thirds played to their lowest-ever crowd, just 297 saw them beat Clydebank

1-0, the club's last victory. They finished 11th in Division Two.

Two weeks later it was announced that Cathkin Park had been offered for sale to Glasgow Corporation for housing. The plan was to move to a new-build stadium, possibly in Bishopbriggs.

Stories of financial irregularities, unpaid players and failings in the club's lottery began to emerge and on June 7, 1967, a winding-up order was issued by the Court of Session. The final straw was a failure to pay for work done on Cathkin Park's grandstand.

Three weeks later, it was announced that Thirds' membership of the Scottish League had ceased. All players were made available for transfer.

Opinions vary on who was to

blame for all this. Investigations were made and the Board of Trade criticised chairman Bill Hiddleston, who was to die of a heart attack in November that year. Other directors were investigated.

The club never revived. The final death throes were so drawn out and tortuous that even the most ardent of supporters had become bone-weary of the endless claim and counterclaim. People drifted away, never to return. A Scottish institution was lost.

■ **The formidable Thirds team of 1960-61. Back, from left: Findlay McGillivray, John Caldwell, Jocky Robertson, Jim Reilly, Jimmy Robb, Willie Cunningham. Front: Jimmy Goodfellow, Dave Hilley, Alex Harley, Matt Gray, Joe McInnes.**

1960~Willie Bauld, the King of Hearts

WILLIE BAULD could head a ball as well as any footballer in history. He was the spearpoint of the famous "Terrible Trio" forward line with Alfie Conn and Jimmy Wardhaugh who propelled Hearts to a rare achievement.

Hearts won seven trophies in the nine seasons from 1954 and finished in the top four 11 seasons in a row. But in 1959-60 they won the League and League Cup in the same season. Aberdeen are the only other club outside the Old Firm to win two trophies in one season.

Willie scored 277 goals for Hearts in 414 games. He died young, aged just 49, in 1977, but is revered by Hearts fans. To this day the Willie Bauld Memorial Club

hold an annual dinner to honour the great man.

■ **Hearts 1960. Back, from left: George Robertson, Danny Ferguson, Andy Bowman, Bobby Kirk, Jim Cruickshank, Wilson Brown, Billy Higgins, Willie Bauld, Archie Kelly, Tommy Henderson. Middle: John Lough, D. Young, Dennis Cunningham, George Thomson, Gordon Smith, Gordon Marshall, Andy Fraser, Jim McFadzean, Jimmy Murray, Alan Finlay. Front: Donald McLeod (trainer), Ian Blackwood, Alex Young, Jimmy Milne, Mr Tommy Walker (manager), John Cumming, Bobby Blackwood, John Hamilton.**

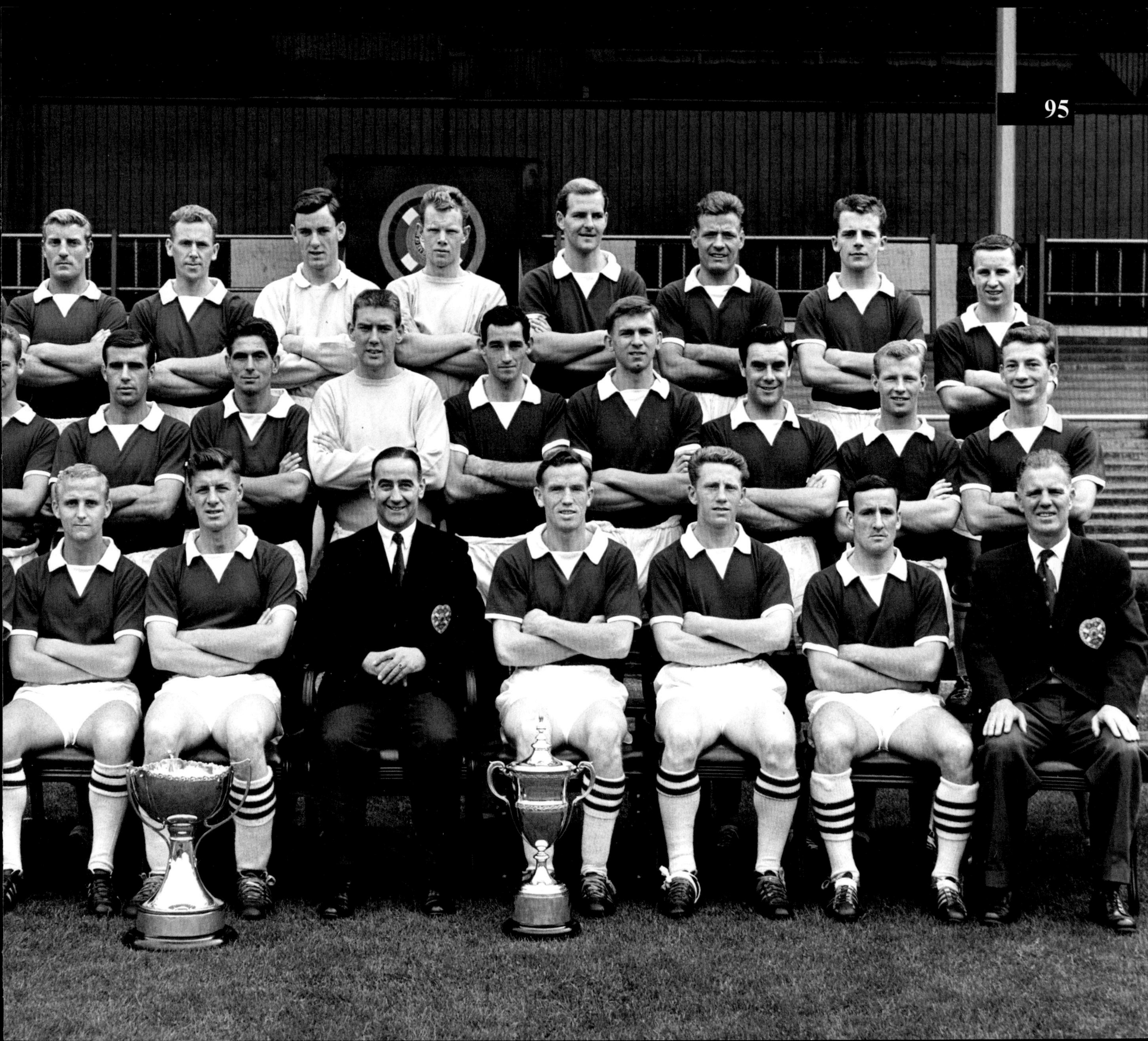

■ **Rangers 1960-61. Back, from left: Stan Anderson, Jimmy Millar, John Currie, Bobby Willie Penman, Andy Matthew, Willie Henderson, Ralph Brand. Middle: Manager Scot McLean, Bill Paterson, Bobby King, Harry Davis, Roger Hynd, Willie Telfer, Dave McMillan, John Queen, Bobby Shearer, Billy Young, Eric Caldow, Donald Bowie, Ian**

Hume, Ron McKinnon, Norrie Martin, George Niven, Billy Ritchie, Bobby Grant, Max Murray, Symon, Albert Franks, Ruben Evans, Billy Stevenson, David More, Sammy Baird, George Provan, Jim Baxter, Joe Craven (assistant trainer). Front: Alex Scott, Willie Cassidy, Ian McColl, Craig Brown, John Little, Craig Watson, Davie Wilson, Davie Kinnear (trainer).

1961~An above Pars performance

WHO wins games? Is it all down to a team's players once they are on the field? Or is it something the manager does? How would you know if your team's manager was any good?

Jock Stein was on his way to becoming a manager of extraordinary skill and perception. He took a Dunfermline team struggling against relegation in the latter part of the 1959-60 season and inspired them to win their final six games.

The next season, 1960-61, he took the club to 12th place, just one place higher than the previous year, not a great improvement. But although adding little to his playing staff, his Pars also won the Scottish Cup for the first time in the club's history.

This picture was taken on April 28, 1961, a league game against Dundee United three days after Dunfermline's 2-0 cup replay win over Celtic. The Pars brought the cup with them and made a few changes to the Hampden line-up. But, mostly, these are the heroes.

■ **From left: Charlie Dickson, John Sweeney, Cammy Fraser, Eddie Connachan, Alex Smith, George Miller, trainer Jimmy Stevenson. Front: George Peebles, Dave Thomson, Ron Mailer, Dan McLindon, Harry Melrose.**

1961~Be fair to Frank Haffey

MANY a legend surrounds Scotland's infamous 9-3 loss to England at Wembley in the Home International meeting of 1961.

Most of those legends are variations on blaming goalkeeper Frank Haffey for the defeat.

That isn't in any way fair, or a true reflection of the game.

It was a terrible performance by Scotland all-round, and they faced a very good England team that also gave Wales and Northern Ireland five-goal beatings in that season's Home Championships. In England's next match after Scotland, they beat Mexico 8-0 and were among the top four seeds for the 1962 World Cup.

Frank was at fault for two of the goals at Wembley, it must be said. But when the score is high, it's usually the goalkeeper who carries the can. The Press went to town on Frank, taking photos beside Big Ben with the hands pointing to nine, and snapping him on his return by rail to Glasgow — at platform 9.

Frank Haffey played for Celtic in the late 1950s and early 1960s, a lean period in the club's history.

He was always a little eccentric. On February 4, 1962, against St Johnstone, he took a quick free-kick close to his goal, and sclaffed the ball into his net (the ref ordered a re-take).

On October 26, 1963, he missed a penalty, although Celtic were 9-0 up at the time and Airdrie 'keeper Roddy McKenzie made a great save — which Frank stood and applauded instead of rushing back to his goal area.

Frank suffered an ankle injury in November 1963 which effectively ended his Celtic career. He had played 201 times, keeping 61 clean sheets.

He moved to Swindon Town, then emigrated to Australia when he was just 26, where he played football but eventually became a cabaret singer, comedian and TV actor.

■ **Celtic, January 14, 1961. Back, from left: John Divers, Billy McNeil, Duncan McKay, Jim Kennedy, Frank Haffey, John Hughes. Front: Charlie Gallacher, Pat Crerand, Bertie Peacock, Stevie Chalmers, Bertie Auld.**

1961~John Greig, the greatest one-club man of them all

RANGERS, the club and the fans, proudly recognise and value tradition, and they revere the great men of their storied history. So to be voted "the greatest ever Ranger" as John Greig was in 1999, is an achievement of note.

Supporters never change their allegiance, so hold a special place in their hearts for players who do the same — men who spend an entire career playing at one club.

Greig made 755 appearances for Rangers, scoring 120 goals, winning three domestic trebles and captaining the side to their 1972 European Cup Winners' Cup victory.

His debut was September 3, 1961, a League Cup tie with Airdrieonians. He scored within 12 minutes. The Sunday Post reported: "*One of the best men on the park was young John Greig. He has the same cool, unhurried approach to the game as Jim Baxter. His passes are studied and nearly always on the ground. And he appears to have all the confidence in the world.*"

But his is a career that cannot be summed up in statistics. John Greig was a leader, an inspiration and a man of great dignity in victory and defeat. His time as a Rangers player coincided with Jock Stein's trophy-laden Celtic side of the mid-1960s to '70s, a time when it was difficult to be a Ranger.

But Greig was undaunted.

He played through those difficult times and emerged to capture the last of the "old" Division One titles, 11 long years after the club's last title win.

When the history of Scottish football is summed up, when the tales of great deeds are told, John Greig's name will be foremost among those mentioned in hushed tones of respect.

■ **John raised on high by his players after Rangers won the 1976 Scottish Cup.**

1962~ Champs Dundee

DUNDEE's free-flowing First Division champions of 1961-62 have been described as one of Scotland's most entertaining sides since the war.

■ **Dundee FC ready to defend their title in the 62-63 season. Back, from left: Gordon Smith, Andy Penman, Bobby Seith, Alex Stuart, Pat Liney, Bobby Wishart, Craig Brown, Bobby Waddell, Lawrie Smith (physio), Alan Gilzean, Ian Ure. Front: Sammy Kean (trainer), Alex Hamilton, Jack Swadel (director), Bobby Cox, James Gellatly (chairman), Alan Cousin, Bob Crighton (director), Hugh Robertson, Bob Shankly (manager).**

106

1962~Can you predict who will be a successful manager?

HOW do you know which young player will go on to make a good football manager?

Did Alex Ferguson look like an inspirational motivator when he joined St Johnstone aged 19? Did Jock Stein show tactical genius when he was a 20-year-old at Albion Rovers?

It's easy to look at these men with hindsight and say "it was always there", but was it obvious at the time?

If the Clyde team of 1962 (left) was examined, then surely Harry Haddock, captain of the side and famously never sent off, booked or even warned by a referee in a 14-year career, would stand out as a managerial candidate. But

the man who did become a fabled boss, Jim McLean, is grinning in the middle row.

McLean, unlike most of the managerial greats didn't show some promise then move to a huge club. Dundee United had never won a trophy when he took over in 1971. Indeed, the club had spent most of its existence in Division Two.

But Jim made them into champions and no team, not Borussia Monchengladbach, Roma, Monaco, Manchester United or, most famously, the mighty Barcelona, could afford to take lightly a Euro draw that paired them with Jim McLean's Dundee United of the 1980s.

To make a small club into a big club is surely as great an achievement as steering a huge club to trophies they should be winning anyway.

■ **Clyde 1962. Back, from left: David White, Moffat, John Finnegan, Harry Haddock, Tommy McCulloch, Donnelly, Dan Currie, Bobby Veitch. Middle: Danny Malloy, Willie Finlay, John McHugh, Tommy Burke, Dick Grant, Jim McLean, Willie McCulloch, Davie Thompson. Front: Graham McFarlane, John McLaughlin, John Divers, Bobby Steel, Ian Blair, John Colrain.**

1962~Younger Fergie's Thistle

THISTLE had put together quite a team for the 1962-63 season. This was the squad of players who recorded 10 victories on the trot that season, including wins over Celtic, Dunfermline and Hibs, on the way to a famous third-place finish behind Rangers and Kilmarnock, one of three occasions (and the most recent) that the club has achieved such a high placing.

This meant qualification for the 1963-64 Fairs Cup the following season.

That 62-63 team included Martin Ferguson, the younger brother of Sir Alex, at inside-forward. Martin had started his career in the Juniors with the famous Kirkintilloch Rob Roy (earning a Scotland Junior cap while there), and would play only 13 games, in total, for The Jags, who were his first senior club. He also played for Morton, Barnsley and Doncaster Rovers.

But he became player-coach of Waterford in the League of Ireland, aged just 27, before managing East Stirlingshire (seven years after his older brother) and Albion Rovers.

In the late 1990s he became his brother's chief European scout, keeping an eye on developing talent across the continent for Manchester United.

The Thistle team of '62-63 also included Davie McParland, a Partick Thistle Hall of Fame member, the man who managed the glorious 1971 promotion and League Cup-winning side. Thistle are to name their new training ground after the great man.

Gordon Whitelaw and Neil Duffy would go on to form a legendary goalscoring combination in the mid-1960s . . . but not at Firhill, they played for St Johnstone by that time.

This photo was taken before an excellent, but very bad-tempered, 3-0 League Cup Group win for the Jags at Pittodrie on August 25, 1962.

■ **Partick Thistle, 1962. Back, from left: Joe Hogan, Sandy Brown, George Niven, Martin Ferguson, John Harvey, Billy Cunningham. Front: Ricky Williamson, Gordon Whitelaw, Billy Hainey, Davie McParland, Neil Duffy.**

1964~Hibs

JOCK STEIN was manager of Hibs for less than a year, but put the club on a firmer footing after they had underperformed during Wally Galbraith's term as boss. Things were looking up at Easter Road.

But Celtic came calling and Jock felt he couldn't say no.

However, statistically, Jock remains Hibs' best-ever manager, with a win rate of 62%.

■ **Back, from left: Eric Stevenson, McMeechan, Davie Hogg, Billy Simpson, Thomson Allan, Bobby Duncan, Derek Whiteford, John Fraser, Willie Hamilton. Middle: Gartshore, George McNeill, Neil Martin, John Parke, Tommy Leishman, Jack Reilly, Willie Wilson, John Baxter, Wilkinson, John McNamee, Jim Easton, manager Jock Stein. Front: assistant trainer Jim Stevenson, Pat Quinn, Jimmy O'Rourke, John Grant, Peter Cormack, Jimmy Stevenson, Stan Vincent, Jim Scott, Cullerton, Pat Stanton, trainer Tom McNiven.**

1964~Morton hero McGraw

ALLAN McGRAW is often given the title "Mr Morton" for his exploits as a player and manager for the Greenock club, and it's a well-deserved name.

He might be better known to younger supporters as a manager of the club for 12 years, 1985 to '97, winning the First Division in 1987 and Second Division in 1995.

But Allan's glory years as a player at Cappielow are really quite remarkable.

He was top scorer in each of his five seasons, 1961-1966, but it is the 63-64 season that stands out.

Govan-born Allan scored a quite incredible 58 goals in 48 games that year, making him the top scorer of any club in Britain.

And all those goals had an effect. Morton got to the League Cup Final of 1963-64 (the final was played in late October '63) in front of 105,000 at Hampden.

As a Second Division club the boys from the tail o the bank had done well to make it to the final but were well-beaten by Rangers, on their way to a clean sweep of Scottish honours that season.

But Morton were unstoppable in their league, winning the Second Division by a comfortable 14 points (in the days of two points for a win).

The club's goals-for tally in the league was 135 in 36 games, a post-war record for the division.

But then, what a team that was. It could boast a young

Joe Harper, Danish imports Kai Johanson and Carl Bertelson, and winger Jimmy Wilson.

The manager was Scottish football's original wheeler-dealer Hal Stewart (see next page).

■ **Morton in 1964. Back, from left: Billy Sinclair, Joe Harper, Ian Henderson, Morris Stevenson, Bobby Adamson. Middle: coach Doug Cowie, Carl Bertleson, Jim Kiernan, John Laughlan, Erik Sorenson, John Boyd, Jimmy Mallon, Hugh Strachan, Dan McKinnon, coach Bobby Howitt. Front: Jim Smart, Kai Johanson, Bobby Campbell, Joe Caven, Allan McGraw, Jimmy Wilson, Willie Laird.**

1965~The Viking invasions

HAL STEWART at Morton and Jerry Kerr, Dundee United's mercurial 1960s manager, were cast in a similar mould.

Hal wasn't strictly a football man. He was a Glasgow-born business tycoon who liked football, gained control of a club and put himself in charge. He didn't often take a big part in training his men, but he certainly had an eye for a player.

Jerry was also a man with an eye for a deal. He had played the game at the top level before making his bones as a manager at Berwick, then Alloa.

His appointment transformed the fortunes of United. He dragged an underperforming club from third bottom of the old Second Division to the top league and on to beating Barcelona home and away in the Fairs Cup.

Stewart and Kerr were men of opportunity.

So when it occurred to them in the early 1960s that the top level of the game in Scandinavia was strictly amateur, they saw an opening. International-class players could be picked up without paying a ha'penny in transfer fees.

And so the Viking invasion of Scottish football began.

Hal brought Danes Kai Johansen, a flying full-back, goalie Erik Sorenson and striker Carl Bertelson to Greenock. He would later sell Johansen and Sorensen to Rangers for tidy sums.

Jerry also raided Denmark, bringing in powerful striker Finn Dossing (who would score 76 goals in 115 games for United) and winger Mogens Berg.

He also grabbed Swedish midfielders Lennart Wing and Orjan Persson. United later sold Persson to Rangers.

Scandinavia would provide many players to Scotland in later years, not least Henrik Larsson and Tore Andre Flo to Celtic and Rangers.

But the original Viking invasion was a huge eye-opener at the time and the players brought in are to this day recalled with great fondness by supporters of the clubs they graced.

■ **United's Scandinavian quartet in 1965. From left: Finn Dossing, Mogens Berg, Orjan Persson, and Lennart Wing.**

1965~Willie's Killie were the real deal

THERE was nothing fortunate about Kilmarnock's league championship win of 1965. They deserved it. Killie had an excellent side and, in Willie Waddell, an inspirational manager.

The former Rangers outside-right was in charge from 1957 until leaving for a job in journalism in 1965. His last act was the incredible final game of the 1964-65 season.

With Killie two points behind Hearts at the top, and one-tenth of a goal worse off on goal-average, they had to beat Hearts 2-0 or better at Tynecastle to win the league.

They duly recorded that 2-0 margin, with first-half goals from Davie Sneddon and Brian McIlroy.

Killie went on to hold the mighty Real Madrid to a 2-2 draw at Rugby Park in the first round of the following season's European Cup.

Waddell would return to football management in 1969 to mastermind Rangers' European Cup-Winners' Cup glory in 1972.

■ **Kilmarnock 1965. Back, from left: Joe Mason, Campbell Forsyth, Ronnie Hamilton. Middle: Pat O'Connor, Eric Murray, Jackie McGrory, Bobby Ferguson, Jim McFadzean, Jack McInally, Frank Malone. Front: Willie Waddell (manager), Hugh Brown, Tommy McLean, Bertie Black, Matt Watson, Frank Beattie, Andy King, Dave Sneddon, Brian McIlroy, Billy Dickson, Walter McCrae (trainer).**

NEVER GO WITHOUT A CAPSTAN

1966~Were they really tougher in the old days?

YES, they were. A penalty had to be the result of a real foul, not just because a player had "felt a touch" in the box. No player would roll over feigning injury — and the game went on in conditions that would horrify (or at least surprise) a modern player.

One of the most famous episodes in Ross County's history, prior to their entry to the national league system, was earned with victory in a snowy cup-tie at Alloa in 1966. County had beaten Forfar in the preliminary

■ Left: February 10, 1966, Highland League County beat Division Two Alloa Athletic. Recreation Park had a covering of snow before the kick-off, and more snow fell during the game. The lines were cleared, though.

round of the Scottish and were drawn to play Alloa away in the first round proper. A Highland League team at the time, County upset The Wasps, and the odds, with a 5-3 victory in a game played in steadily falling snow. None of the players wore tights.

The reward was a home tie with Rangers, scheduled for February 20.

Thousands travelled from Glasgow to Dingwall for the game, including a seven-carriage special train, but a snowstorm even worse than the one 10 days before had engulfed the entire north of Scotland.

The game couldn't go ahead, but the huge contingent of Rangers fans had an enjoyable, if cold, day out in the Highland town. Cafes and shops sold out of food, and pubs were 10-deep at the bar.

Continued overleaf.

1966~A game that had consequences

There was talk of the Rangers team staying overnight in Inverness, with an eye on playing the game on the Sunday — but that would have required an unlikely thaw. Despite both clubs having had games the previous Saturday, the postponed tie went ahead on the afternoon of Monday, February 28. Rangers won 2-0 and would win the cup that year.

The excitement of Rangers visiting the Highlands had a far-reaching consequence.

A 12-year-old laddie named Roy McGregor was at the game and fell in love with football in general and Ross County in particular. Years later, when he had become a successful businessman, he would take on the role of chairman of the club and provide the financial foundation that County's rise to the top level of the Scottish game was built upon.

■ Right: The Ross County team that won at Alloa. Back, from left: Peter Borley, Colin Brett, Benny Sutherland, Ian McNeill, Ian Greig, Dom McMillan. Front: Tommy Thomson, Sandy MacKenzie, Denis Donald, Jim Hosie, John Mackay.

1966~Team Bobby

IT would be unfair to pick out any one man from the Celtic team of the 1965 to 75 era. Each had a different job and each was highly accomplished at his task. But it is possible to take a man in isolation and examine his attributes.

Bobby Murdoch had a talent that went beyond individual skill. He was quite the player himself, of course, two-footed, resolute in the tackle and able to find a pass when doing so looked impossible. The perfect all-round midfielder.

But what sets Bobby apart is that he made players around him better.

He gave them the ball when they were best placed to receive it and got them out of trouble when they most needed it.

He excelled at one of the more difficult-to-define parts of the game, the art of teamwork.

Bobby provided the canvas upon which the strokes of individual brilliance could be drawn. A great team man in a great team is the most powerful force in football.

■ **Celtic 1966. Back, from left: George Connelly, Tommy Gemmell, Ian Young, John Cushley, John Divers, Steve Chalmers, Charlie Gallagher, Jim Brogan. Middle: Manager Jock Stein, John Hughes, Billy McNeill, Bent Martin, John Kennedy, Ronnie Simpson, John Fallon, Frank McCarron, Bobby Murdoch, Willie O'Neil; assistant manager Sean Fallon. Front: trainer Bob Rooney, Jimmy Johnstone, Joe McBride, Henry McQuinn, Dave Cattenach, John Clark, Bertie Auld, Bobby Lennox, coach Neil Mochan.**

1966~Bobby, and all those tempted south

BOBBY SEITH, seen here in his later role at Dens Park as a member of the backroom staff, is a good example of what the English leagues have done with Scottish players for many a decade. Bobby was born and raised in Scotland but in 1948, as a 16-year-old, was scouted by the then up-and-coming Burnley side and spent the first 12 years of his career in Lancashire.

The model wasn't new in 1948 when Bobby signed for Burnley, and would be repeated again and again through the years.

Scotland produced great players — Law, Bremner, Hartford, Wark, Busby, Shankly, to name a few — who were lured south as kids. A few, like Bobby Seith, would eventually

come home, but the Scottish game was always poorer for the constant drain of its young talent.

■ **Dundee FC 1966-67. Back, from left: Jocky Scott, Davie Swan, Alex Bryce, John Arrol, Ally Donaldson, Jim Easton, Steve Murray, John Duncan. Middle: Bobby Seith (trainer), Ron Selway, Bobby Wilson, Sammy Wilson, B. Andon, Doug Houston, George Stewart, Alex Kinninmonth, M. Goodall, J. Syme, Bobby Ancell (manager), G. Stevenson (physio). Front: Derek McKay, Tony Harvey, Andy Penman, Alex Hamilton, Jim Mclean, Bobby Cox, Norrie Beattie, Kenny Cameron, R. Campbell, Alex Stuart, Bobby Rough.**

1966~The unexpected victory

THERE is victory, and then there is a victory when you didn't think your team had much of a chance. The second type is by far the more enjoyable.

Dundee United have played the mighty Barcelona four times in European competition — Fairs Cup ties in 1966 and UEFA Cup meetings in 1987 — and have beaten the Spanish giants in all four games.

They grabbed an unlikely 2-1 victory in the Nou Camp on October 25, 1966, becoming the first British club to win a European tie on Spanish soil. But most "experts" reckoned the United underdogs still had a lot of work to do in the Inter Cities Fairs Cup return leg on November 16, 1966.

The match captured the imagination of the local support. An all-ticket 28,000 (still United's record attendance) squeezed into Tannadice for the game.

United had that huge crowd in raptures, however, with an unexpectedly assured performance.

They won 2-0 on the night with strikes from Ian Mitchell and Billy Hainey, had a further two "goals" disallowed and Belgian ref Robert Schaut refused what looked a stonewall penalty when Tommy Miller was brought down in the box.

The crowd celebrated long and loud in the streets of Dundee after the game, while the team raised a few bottles themselves (and smoked a few fags) in the dressing room.

That unexpected, against-the-odds, victory feeling is rare, but many a Scottish team has experienced it — several have an entry in their "honours won" list to mark the occasion.

It is those victories which are among the most cherished, most fondly-remembered, among supporters.

■ **Dundee United's players pose for a victory photo in the Tannadice dressing room after beating Barcelona in 1966. Back, from left: Jimmy Briggs, Tommy Neilson, Doug Smith, Lennart Wing, Sandy Davie, Billy Hainey. Front: Finn Seemann, Tommy Millar, Dennis Gillespie, Ian Mitchell. Orjan Persson, who also played, is not pictured.**

■ Celtic 1966-67. Back, from left: Jim Brogan, Willie O'Neill, Ian Young, John Cushley, Tommy Gemmell, Jim Craig, Davie Cattenach, Charlie Gallacher, Tony Taylor, Jim Clark. Middle: Coaches John Higgins and Neil Mochan, Brian Goodwin, Jimmy Quinn, John Clark, John Hughes, Bent Martin, John Fallon, Ronnie Simpson, John Kennedy, Frank McCarron, John Halpin, Sam Henderson, David Hay, trainer Bob Rooney and assistant manager Sean Fallon.

■ **Front: Public relations officer Jimmy McGrory, director Tom Devlin, John Taggart, Jimmy Johnstone, Stevie Chalmers, Joe McBride, Billy McNeill, chairman Bob Kelly, Bobby Murdoch, Bobby Lennox, Bertie Auld, Lou Macari, John Gorman, secretary Desmond White, manager Jock Stein. Trophies: Ibrox Disaster Cup, Victory Cup, St Mungo Cup, Coronation Cup, League Championship, League Cup, Second XI Cup, Empire Exhibiton Trophy, Glasgow Cup.**

1967~The best there will ever be

NO matter which team they support, a fair-minded football fan would have to admit that Celtic winning the European Cup with 11 players born within 20 miles of Celtic Park, is the greatest achievement of any team in world football history. It is a badge of honour for Scotland, as well as the club.

This is a feat that will never be, can never be, surpassed.

Yes, the game was different back then. It was slower, perhaps less tactically-astute. And modern scientific training methods have made players fitter. But it was different for all teams. Celtic's win cannot be decried unless Real Madrid's glories are to be similarly downgraded, or Brazil's maestros of 1970 are to be criticised.

Even in the partisan, divided atmosphere of Scottish football, it must be acknowledged that this was our nation's greatest ever triumph.

The crowning point to be made is that Celtic didn't scrape past Inter Milan, they easily beat the team that had won two of the past three European Cups. The 2-1 scoreline flattered the Italians.

■ **The return to Celtic Park with the trophy.**

1967~You don't have to be tall to make yourself a big name

ASK a Stirling Albion fan who their bright young star of the sixties was. Ask a St Johnstone supporter who the hero of the club's 1970s European adventures was. Ask a Dundee United man who the club's most exciting signing of 1975 was...the answer will be the same for all of those questions — Henry Hall.

Manager Willie Ormond broke St Johnstone's transfer fee record to snatch Henry from Stirling Albion. Jim McLean eventually tempted him to Tannadice in Dundee United's quest to find a replacement for Andy Gray.

There is a good reason why two of the great managers of the 1970s were so keen to have Henry Hall in their team.

It was nothing to do with stature. Much is made of the fact that Henry wasn't the tallest player who ever stood on a football pitch. As if that mattered. A high proportion of Scotland's best players haven't been giants.

The reason Henry Hall was so sought after was that he was wonderfully adept at doing the most important thing in the game — putting the ball in the net.

His secret when doing this wasn't complicated, but is incredibly rare. Henry's great talent lay in his cool and calculating composure in front of goal. He wouldn't win many headers, he didn't go in for much long-range shooting. But give him the ball in a crowded penalty box and he'd get in a well-struck effort on goal. Managers really like that sort of thing.

Henry is seen on the right with his future St Johnstone team-mate Alex Rennie.

■ **Stirling Albion 1967. Back, from left: Willie Cunningham, Willie Murray, Walter Myles, Alex Rennie, Drew Rogerson, Billy Reid. Front: Danny McKinnon, Matt McPhee, Bob Murray, Jim Kerray, George Peebles, Henry Hall.**

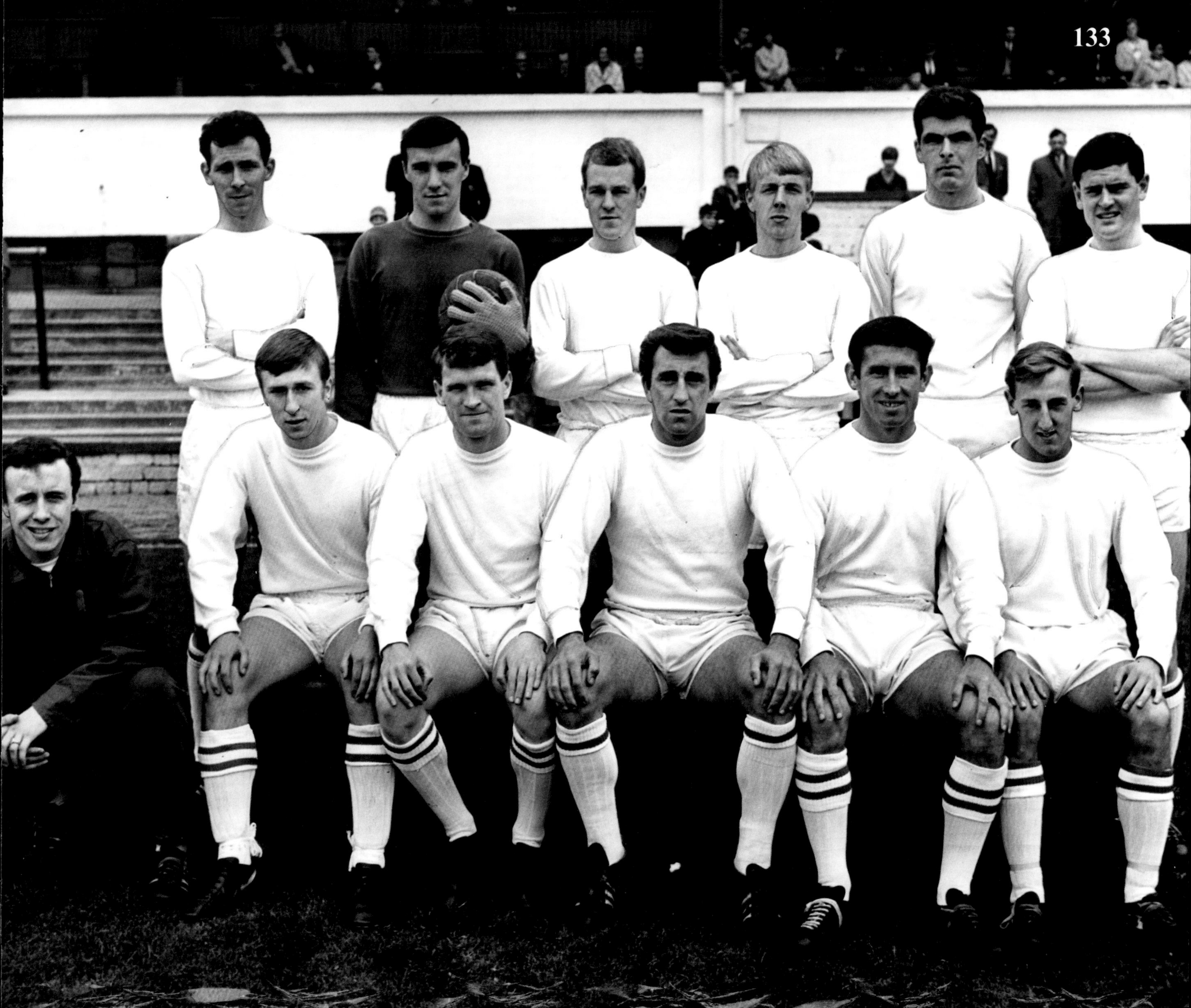

1967~Scotland's best uncapped player?

IT's one thing scoring goals in a team that is at the top of the league, it's quite another to get a barrow-load of goals in a team fighting relegation.

Gordon Wallace was the first non-Old Firm player to win the Football Writers' Player of the Year award, in 1967-68. He scored 30 league goals for a team that finished one place above the relegation zone and only scored 58 goals in total.

Wallace put the ball in the net wherever he played, as a lad at Montrose, in Raith Rovers' promotion-winning side of 1966-67, at Dundee, Dundee United and Seattle Sounders.

He scored the goal that won the League Cup for Dundee in 1973, the club's last major silverware.

He was never capped for Scotland.

You'll have an opinion on who Scotland's best uncapped player was. Every fan does. A man who scores in difficult circumstances, though, would surely have been worth a run out?

Alongside him in this Raith Rovers line-up is Ian Porterfield, who would score the goal that won the 1973 FA Cup for Sunderland, and former Celtic captain and legend Bobby Evans.

■ **The Raith team that beat Stirling Albion 7-1 on September 23, 1967. Back, from left: Jocky Richardson (sub), Bobby Stein, Bobby Reid, Alex Gray, Bobby Kinloch, Bobby Evans, Ian Porterfield, J. Fraser (trainer). Front: Ian Lister, Davie Sneddon, Gordon Wallace, Jim Murphy, Geordie Falconer.**

1967~Giantkillers

SAMMY REID was Bill Shankly's first signing when he became manager of Liverpool. The then 21-year-old Reid had been a star inside-forward for Motherwell.

He never played a game for The Reds, however, but went on to become a free-scoring striker for Falkirk, then Clyde, before a transfer to Berwick Rangers at the start of the 1966-67 season.

And it is this second spell south of the Border (though not far south of it) for which he is most famous.

In the 32nd minute of a 1967 Scottish Cup tie with Glasgow Rangers, Sammy's left-foot shot went into the net off the inside of keeper Norrie Martin's post — and caused the biggest upset in the competition's history.

The Big Rangers were cup holders and second top of the First Division. The Wee Rangers were part-timers and tenth in Division Two.

But Sammy's strike was the only goal of the game.

He had to quickly come back down to earth. After taking time off for training in the lead-up to the cup-tie, the day after the great win Sammy had to work a Sunday shift at his job as a gear-cutter in an engineering yard.

■ **Back, from left: Gordon Haig, Jim Kilgannon, Jock Wallace, Russell Craig, Ian Riddell, Andy Rogers. Front: Tommy Lumsden, Kenny Dowds, Doug Coutts, George Christie, Sammy Reid, Alan Ainslie.**

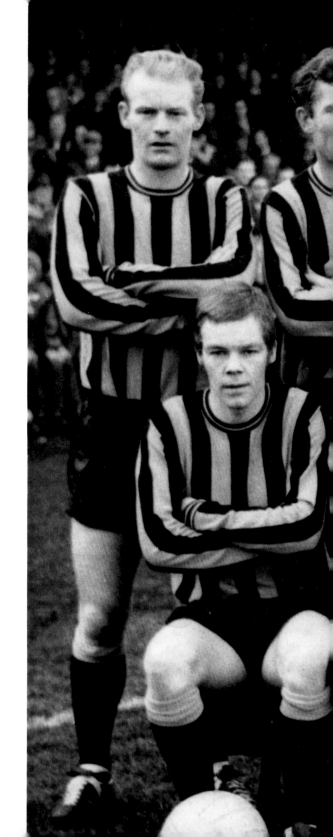

1967~The scapegoats

FOR every hero, there is a villain. The Rangers supporters in the 13,000 crowd at Shielfield were far from happy with the first time Rangers had ever lost to a lower-league club.

The pavilion was beseiged after the game, bottles were thrown as the mob called for Rangers manager Scott Symon to resign. Police formed a human barrier to keep the peace.

But the men who paid for the biggest upset in Scottish Cup history were strikers Jim Forrest and George McLean. Neither ever played for Rangers again.

Forrest was 22 and had played 163 games for the club, scoring a quite incredible 145 goals.

He went to Preston, then came back north to spend five years at Aberdeen, where he was part of their 1970 cup-winning side.

McLean went to Dundee, where he earned a Scotland cap in 1968.

■ **Below, the final whistle at Shielfield on January 28, 1967.**

1968~The benefits of good recruitment

THE Dunfermline set-up of the 1960s stands as a blueprint for what a club from a provincial town can achieve in the modern game with good organisation and good management.

This was their second Scottish Cup win, in their third final of the 1960s. They played more than 40 European ties throughout the decade.

The secret is that The Pars had three good managers in a row, Jock Stein, Willie Cunningham and George Farm. It isn't often a club's board of directors are given credit, but this was a triumph in the art of employee selection.

Dunfermline's play in the '68 final was the brightest light in this golden period, and stands as fitting tribute to the club's superb organisation, continuity and skill in recruitment.

Dunfermline met Hearts in that 1968 final and saw them off with relative ease, 3-1.

■ **Back, from left: Andy Stevenson (physio), Tom Callaghan, John McGarty, Jim Fraser, Bent Martin, Willie Duff, Barrie Mitchell, Bert Paton, Willie Renton, Bob Methven (assistant trainer). Middle: Ian Cowan, Ian Lister, Willie Callaghan, Jim Thomson, Barry, Robertson, Alec Totten, Alec Edwards. Front: Eddie Ferguson, George McKimmie, Pat Gardner, John Lunn.**

1968~Prince Kenny

IT is often a waste of time to examine Scottish football records, just take it that whatever record you are looking for is held by Kenny Dalglish.

Most caps, most international goals, the only man to have won all three domestic trophies north and south of the Border, plus three European Cups.

Not a bad player, all in all.

He started, however, as a member of Celtic's Quality Street Gang, the reserve players pushing through into the club's nine-in-a-row team in the late 1960s.

This photo shows the Celtic squad of 1968, both the "greats" of the first team and kids like Danny McGrain and Lou Macari who would soon become huge stars in their own right.

This was 17-year-old Kenny's first season as a full-time player, having been farmed out to Cumbernauld United, and a joinery apprenticeship, the previous year.

■ Celtic 1968. Back, from left: Jim Brogan, Danny McGrain, Joe McBride, Davie Cattanach, George Connelly, John Fallon, Ronnie Simpson, Charlie Gallagher, Jimmy Quinn, John Clark, Kenny Dalglish, Willie O'Neill. Middle: Bobby Wraith, John Hughes, Davie Hay, Jim Craig, Jacky Clarke, Tommy Gemmell, Hugh McKellar, Bobby Murdoch, John Murray, Stevie Chalmers, Tom Livingstone. Front: Pat McMahon, Jimmy Johnstone, Lou Macari, Willie Wallace, Vic Davidson, Billy McNeill, Paul Wilson, Bobby Lennox, Jim Clarke, Bertie Auld, John Gorman.

1968~No regrets

THEY called him the new George Best and the label was quite apt. Peter Marinello was very good at football and very good at drinking. By Peter's own admission, he just couldn't say no. Money, glamour, stardom, being Arsenal's first six-figure signing — when you had talent and looks like his in the late 1960s and early '70s, it all seemed natural.

He scored a memorable goal against Manchester United on his 1970 Arsenal debut, taking the break of the ball before cutely dummying his way round United stalwart Tony Dunne and slotting the ball into the net. It looked like The Gunners had, indeed, found their own Georgie Best.

But too many drinks in his hand and too many kicks to his knee saw him transferred to Portsmouth, in the Second Division, in 1973, then Motherwell in 1975. After short-lived contracts in Australia and America he signed for Hearts in 1981. A bad investment in a Spanish bar saw him eventually declared bankrupt.

However, in true Scottish maverick style, when asked, long after retirement, if he'd have changed anything, Peter would speak only of the good times.

He was, in truth, a magnificently talented footballer and the Easter Road crowd probably saw the best of him.

■ Hibs 1968-1969. From left: Pat Quinn, Eric Stevenson, Jimmy O'Rourke, Billy Simpson, Allan McGraw, Chris Shevlane, Peter Marinello, Joe Davis, John Blackley, Peter Cormack, Colin Stein, Alex Scott, Willie Wilson, Thomson Allan, Pat Stanton, Murray, Alan Cousin, Ian Wilkinson.

146

1969~Goal-machine and goal-stopper

JOHN DEANS was given the nickname "Dixie" in reference to his namesake William Dean, the Everton goalscoring great of the 1920s and '30s.

Both men were incredibly prolific.

The Scottish Dixie started his career with Motherwell in 1965 and played 152 games over six seasons, rattling in 78 goals before going on to become a Celtic great.

At the other end of the pitch stood the towering figure of Peter McCloy in goal, "The Girvan Lighthouse", who would go on to become a Rangers legend.

But in 1969-70, 'Well had the nucleus of a good side. The ever-dependable Joe Wark and Willie McCallum at the back, the bite of Tam Forsyth (not in this photo) in midfield, and the powerful John Goldthorp and Jackie McInally (father of Alan who would play for Ayr United, Celtic and Bayern Munich) up front.

■ **Motherwell 1969. Back, from left: Jim Muir, Davie Whiteford, Joe Wark, Tom Donnelly, Peter McCloy, Willie McCallum, John Murray. Front: Bobby Howitt (manager), Jimmy Wilson, Jackie McInally, Billy Campbell, Dixie Deans, John Goldthorp, Wilson Humphries (coach).**

■ Elgin City skipper Doug Grant chaired by his team mates after the club won the 1970 Qualifying Cup.

■ **Inverness Caley, Highland League Champions 1971. Back, from left: H. Munro (trainer), F. Neild, D. Park, S. Forsyth, C. Allan, M. Slater, K. MacGregor, R. Mackintosh (vice president). Middle: D. Lowrie, senior vice-president, J. Lynas, D. Lockhart, A. Anderson, R. Noble, K. Mackenzie, D. Bennett. Front: N. Smith (secretary), A. Presslie (captain), J. McPherson (chairman), D. Johnston, A. Veighey (treasurer).**

1971~Teen DJ

SUPPORTERS love it when their club brings through a player from the youth system who explodes on to the scene. There has rarely been an explosion of such magnitude as the one set off by Derek Johnstone.

DJ signed for Rangers at the age of 14 and was just 16 when he was given a start in the 1971 League Cup Final.

He had played only three senior games before that, starting only one of them. But he repaid the faith of manager Willie Waddell by getting up to bullet home a header in the 40th minute, which turned out to be the only goal of the game.

Derek's aerial prowess made him equally adept when playing as a centre-half. He is still the only player to have been selected for Scotland as a striker, midfielder and defender.

■ **Rangers 1971. Back, from left: Alfie Conn, Colin Stein, George Donaldson, Gerhardt Neef, Peter McCloy, Colin Jackson, Bobby Watson, D. Stevenson, Graham Fyfe, Iain McDonald. Middle: Jock Wallace, Tom Craig, Kenny Watson, Willie Mathieson, Renton, Ron McKinnon, Alex Miller, Sandy Jardine, Derek Johnstone, Dave Smith, Gus McCallum, Joe Craven, Stan Anderson (assist. coach). Front: Willie Waddell, Willie Henderson, Billy Semple, Alex MacDonald, Tom Alexander, John Greig, Derek Parlane, Andy Penman, Morrison, Willie Johnston, Willie Thornton.**

1971~Your country is your country

JOE BAKER was born in 1940 in Liverpool, to an English father and Scottish mother. He moved to Motherwell at the age of six weeks and there he stayed.

This wouldn't be a problem for most people. But Joe was different, he was a very good footballer, a goalscoring Hibees star.

As far as Joe thought, he was Scottish, and played for the Scotland Schools team. But when it came to playing for a senior international team, the rules said he was English.

So Joe became the first man to play for England who had never played football in England. He won six under-23 caps and eight full caps, only narrowly missing selection for the 1966 World Cup squad.

Nowadays, the rules are different.

Players play for the nations of far-flung relatives. It was simpler, some would say better, in the old days. You played for your country of birth.

■ Hibs 1971. Back, from left: **Arthur Duncan, Chris Shevlane, Jim Black, Price, Roy Baines, Gillet, John Brownlie, Joe Baker, John Fraser (asst. trainer). Middle: T. McNiven (trainer), Mathieson, Jimmy O'Rourke, Pat Stanton, Colin Grant, Alan Gordon, John Blackley, Miller, John Hazel, Dennis Nelson, Eddie Turnbull (manager). Front: Kenny Davidson, Alex Pringle, Johnny Graham, Johnny Hamilton, Billy McEwan, Erich Schaedler, Alex Cropley, Bertie Auld, John Young, Eric Stevenson.**

1971~Teddy Scott. Not all heroes are players

TEDDY SCOTT played one first-team game for Aberdeen FC, which doesn't usually qualify for Hall of Fame status.

He was a football man, he won a Scottish Junior Cup medal with Sunnybank in 1954 before signing for The Dons. And though opportunities in Dave Halliday's all-conquering team were limited, Teddy had found a home for life.

His duties were varied over the course of serving 11 managers, but he took training, looked after the kit, gave the young lads advice, and grew to be one of the club's best-loved, hardest-working and most-respected back-room men.

Members of the Red Army tell of meeting him during tours of Pittodrie. Each tale ends with an account of a friendly chat and agreement on what a great bloke he was. Every club should have an ambassador like Teddy Scott.

■ **Aberdeen 1971. Back, from left: Bobby Clark, Henning Boel, George Murray, Tommy McMillan, Martin Buchan, Tommy Wilson, Sandy Clelland, Dave Robb, Joe Smith, Andy Geoghegan. Middle: Jim Hamilton, Ian Taylor, Jim Hermiston, Willie Young, Billy Williamson, Chic McLelland, Bertie Miller, Ian Purdie, Jim Smith, Arthur Graham, George Lindsay, Graham Ross. Front: physio Ronnie Coutts, Steve Murray, John Craig, Jim Forrest, Charlie Elvin, Alex Willoughby, Jimmy Bonthrone, Andy Kerr, Joe Harper, Ian Hair, George Buchan, trainer Teddy Scott.**

1971~The other Hansen

JOHN HANSEN might have formed one of the great defensive partnerships not just at Firhill but in the Scotland team, with his younger brother Alan, if it hadn't been for cruel injury problems.

John was a member of the Thistle side relegated from the First Division in 1970, but which bounced back as Second Division champions in 1971.

The brothers played for Sauchie Juniors before having four seasons together for Thistle.

John won two Scotland caps in 1972, but various knee ops put a stop to a proposed big-money transfer to Manchester United and would ultimately force him into retirement aged just 27.

He was a member of the team that caused one of the biggest upsets in Scottish football history, the humbling of the powerful nine-in-a-row Celtic side in the 1971 League Cup Final.

Thistle were four up by the 37th minute and, legend has it, the crowd was then swelled by Rangers supporters, hearing on the radio of their rivals being beaten, flocking to the ground. Celtic pulled a goal back in the second half, but it was Thistle's day.

The Jags were applauded off the field by the Celtic players, and many Celtic supporters, as well as the Thistle fans.

■ **The Thistle team that won the 1971 League Cup was: Alan Rough, John Hanson, Alex Forsyth, Ronnie Glavin, Jackie Campbell, Hugh Strachan, Denis McQuade, Frank Coulston, Jimmy Bone, Alex Rae, Bobby Lawrie and Johnny Gibson.**

1972~Lichted Up

THE 1970s was a good decade for The Red Lichties. They narrowly missed promotion to the First Division in 1970-71 but made the jump the following season.

This is the team (right) that took second place behind Dumbarton in the Second Division, but with the same number of points. This was the season that goal difference replaced goal average in Scotland, and the placings would have been the same under either system — but if goal average had still been in place, it might have been a more exciting end to the campaign.

Goal average was calculated by dividing the number of goals scored by goals conceded. Dumbarton's GA would have been 1.745. Arbroath's GA would have been 1.731. They would have needed to have scored just one more goal to pip The Sons to the title.

But the old system had been swept away and Arboath were promoted anyway.

And rightly so, because they had quite a team under Bert Henderson, manager for 18 years 1962-1980, spending four of those seasons in the top division.

■ **Arbroath 1972. Back, from left: manager Bert Henderson, Jim Milne, Derek McKay, Tom Cargill, Terry Wilson, Bobby Waddell, Derek Rylance, trainer Johnny Martin. Front: Eric Sellars, Jim Cant, Billy Pirie, John Fletcher, Kenny Payne, Hugh Robertson.**

1972~A national hero

ALLY MacLEOD was inducted into the Scottish Football Hall of Fame in 2015. He thoroughly deserved the honour.

Anyone who recalls the heady days of 1977 and the first half of 1978, when Ally took enthusiasm for the national team to the greatest ever heights, must look back on that time with nothing but fondness.

We believed, we were ambitious. We were on the march with Ally's Army, united behind the team to a degree not seen since.

Those years were surely the zenith of the famous "Wha's like us?" Scottish mentality.

We didn't have the best of tournaments at Argentina '78, it is true to say. But it should be remembered that Ally was very good at his job. He got Scotland through a qualifying group for that World Cup that contained 1976 European champions Czechoslovakia.

He won the League Cup as boss of Aberdeen.

He is also remembered as possibly the best manager in Ayr United's history. He made The Honest Men a solid top-division side and took them to the semi-finals of both national cup competitions.

Before that, as a talented left-winger, he was Blackburn Rovers' man-of-the-match in the 1960 FA Cup final, though they lost 3-0 to Wolves.

A man of the people, he played a prominent part (along with Jimmy Hill) in getting the maximum wage system in England abolished.

It's surely impossible not to love Ally.

■ **Ayr United 1972-73. Back, from left: Bobby Tait, Davie Wells, J. Jackson, Alex McAnespie, David Stewart, Jim McFadzean, Rikki Fleming, George McLean, Jim Flynn. Middle: W. Wallace (trainer), Brian Lannon, Stan Quinn, Ian Campbell, Joe Filippi, Ally McLean, Alex McGregor, G. Greir, John Murphy, Phil McGovern, W. McCulloch (trainer). Front: Davie Robertson, Bobby Rough, Johnny Doyle, Doug Mitchell, Sam McMillan (coach), Alex Ingram, Ally MacLeod (manager), Johnny Graham, H. Thomson, Tommy Reynolds, Davie McCulloch.**

1972~Pat Stanton, a man for the big game

FOOTBALL managers like nothing better than a player who steps up on the big occasion. Consistency wins a league, the gladiator who is at his best in a life or death game is what wins cups.

A Fairs Cup tie against Napoli in 1967, when Hibs were 4-1 down after the first leg is a great example. The Pat Stanton-inspired fightback saw off the Italians 5-0 at Easter Road, with Pat scoring the fourth with a bullet header.

The Famous Five had taken two league championships in the 1950s but Hibs hadn't won a cup since 1902. Pat, and the great team he played in, changed that.

The 1972 League Cup Final was Pat's crowning glory. He opened the scoring on the hour and crossed for Jim O'Rourke's second to beat Celtic 2-1.

■ Hibs 1972. Back, from left: Alex McGhee, James Reynolds, Arthur Duncan, Ray Hardie; John Minford, Hugh White, Bobby Robertson, Jim McArthur, John Salton, Gerry Adair, Jim Black, David McMillan, Alex Cropley. Middle: Robert Smith, Willie Murray, John Hazel, James Callan, John Blackley, Tony Higgins, Alex McGregor, John Brownlie, Derek Spalding, Jimmy O'Rourke, Dave Wallace, Kenny Davidson. Front: Alex Edwards, Billy Muldoon, Steven McLaughlin, Des Bremner, Erich Schaedler, Iain Munro, Pat Stanton, Alan Gordon, Les Thomson, John Williams, Lawrence Dunn, Ian Miller, Peter Douglas.

1973~Recognition, the Fitzpatrick Way

WHO among us can say our name will live for ever? The 17-year-old Anthony Fitzpatrick in this photo, right at the start of his career, couldn't have known he would become a St Mirren legend.

But he has had a street, "Fitzpatrick Way" named after him on the site of the old Love Street ground, which has been redeveloped as affordable housing, Tony will indeed be remembered for ever.

It is a fitting tribute to a man who has given so much of his life as a player, manager and chief executive to a club he clearly loves.

Well done Paisley. Every town, should immortalise the names of its heroes.

■ St Mirren, 1973. Back, from left: Henry Mowbray, Alistair Lafferty, Graham Hart, Jim Herriot, Scott McKay, Tony Fitzpatrick, Paul Stewart. Middle: John Fulton, John Dickson, Sandy Cleland, Brian Third, Jason Walker, Richard McLachlan, Wilson Lamb, John Jamieson, David Millar. Front: Willie Cunningham (manager), Bobby McKean, Gus McLeod, Billy Johnston, Jim Taylor, Dave Robertson, Duncan McGill (trainer).

1973~ Hearts

■ Hearts 1973. Back, from left: Peter Oliver, Ian Sneddon, Alan Anderson, David Graham, Kenny Garland, Jimmy Cruickshank, John Gallacher, Jim Cant, Eric Carruthers. Middle: Bobby Seith (manager), Jim Brown, Dave Clunie, Davie Dick, Roy Kay, John McKay, Harry Kinnear, Jim Jeffries, Drew Busby, Willie Gibson, John Cumming (trainer), John Haggart (asst. trainer). Front: Donald Ford, Bobby Conn, Tommy Murray, John Stevenson, Kenny Aird, Alan Wilson, Gordon Welsh, Donald Park, Ralph Callachan. Sitting: Dumayne, Hoggan, Noble, Hepson, McMillan, Darling, Tom Harvey, Willie Gibson, Finlayson.

1973~A braw player, long before Pele quip

THERE was only ever one John Lambie. The larger-than-life manager of (most notably) Partick Thistle is held in unique respect in Scottish football.

John's "tell him his name is Pele" quip is so famous it needs no further explanation, and he swore so much he sometimes broke up swearwords to insert another swearword between the syllables.

But before John was a cigar-smoking, pigeon-fancying, old-school manager he was a tenacious full-back and an immensely popular figure with the fans of Falkirk (1958-69) and St Johnstone (69-74).

John was a key member of the Saints side that reached the 1969 League Cup final and beat German giants Hamburg in the first round of the 1971-72 UEFA Cup.

■ St Johnstone 1973. Back, from left: Billy Ritchie, Jimmy Argue, Dave Cochrane, Jim Donaldson, Sandy Smith, John Hotson, Atholl Henderson. Middle: John McQuade, Billy McManus, G. Campbell, Fred Aitken, Derek Robertson, Andy Kinnell, Lindsay Hamilton, Alex Rennie, D. Kerr. Front: I. Bateman, Gordon Smith, Gordon McGregor, John Muir, B. Easton, Benny Rooney, Ross Jenkins, Jim Pearson, Bobby Thomson, John Lambie, R. Smethurst.

1973~Larger-than-life Jim Leishman

THE job requirements for being a manager would require any candidate to have personality. Being inspirational would help. Being a larger-than-life Fifer might be useful too. In other words, be Jim Leishman.

Jim's career as a player was curtailed by injury. He played only 91 games over seven years after signing as an S-form for The Pars in 1970.

In 1982, aged 28, he became the club's youngest ever manager.

Dunfermline were bottom of the Scottish football league system, but Jim got them to the Premier Division within four years. Along the way he recited poetry, indulged in areoplane-arms goal celebrations, and became a hugely popular figure with the Pars fans.

■ **Dunfermline 1973. Back, from left: Jim Scott, Gordon Pate, Joe Hughes, David Petrie, Billy Mitchell, Willie Tempany, Jim Gillespie, Gordon Forrest, Dave McNicoll, Ian Campbell, Dennis Nelson. Middle: John Thompson, Sammy Beresford, Jim Wallace, J. Docherty, John Arrol, Graham Shaw, George Thomson, Allan Evans, Jim Leishman, Charlie Brine, Jim Thomson. Front: George Miller (manager), Robert Hamill, Jim Brown, Kenny Thomson, Jim Markey, Alex Kinninmonth, Robert Cameron, Ken Mackie, Jackie Sinclair, Kenny Watson, Andy Stevenson.**

1973~Silver can be a scarce commodity

SUPPORTING a provincial club isn't easy. Years, decades, sometimes generations can pass between silverware being lifted.

Hearts last won the league in 1960, Motherwell haven't won it since 1932. There were 114 years between Hibs' two most recent Scottish Cup wins.

Partick last won the Scottish Cup in 1921, and the League Cup in 1971, with nothing since.

East Fife haven't won a national competition since 1953; Dumbarton haven't won one of the top trophies since 1892.

Lower league cups and titles come along every so often, but are morsels compared to the feasts when a proper piece of silverware is lifted. It can be, indeed, a hard life following a "wee" club.

Dundee's last major trophy was the League Cup of 1973-74 (the final was played on December 15, 1973). They have been to League and Scottish Cup finals in the years since, but haven't won one.

■ **The Dundee squad toast their 1973 League Cup victory in the city's long-since demolished Angus Hotel. The cup-winning team was: Thomson Allan, Jimmy Wilson, Tommy Gemmell, Bobby Ford, George Stewart, Iain Phillip, John Duncan, Bobby Robinson, Gordon Wallace, Jocky Scott, Duncan Lambie. Subs: Davie Johnston, Ian Scott.**

1975~Almost Scottish Leeds

MANY clubs in England have a long history of fielding Scottish players. A team (prior to the Premier League era) winning the English First Division without a Scotsman in the ranks was a rare thing.

Leeds United's celebrated teams of the 1960s and '70s had a strong Scottish core. Their team that played the 1975 European Cup Final featured six Scotsmen.

This Leeds line-up, from 1975-76, has 15 players. Eight of them are Scottish, all eight were capped for Scotland.

Leeds' "glory years", (roughly 1960 to 1976) coincide almost exactly with the span of that proudest of Scots, Billy Bremner's, career at Elland Road.

Wha's like us in Yorkshire?

■ **Leeds United 1975: Back, from left: Manager Jimmy Armfield, Duncan McKenzie, Joe Jordan, Gordon McQueen, David Harvey, David Stewart, Paul Madeley, Norman Hunter, Paul Reaney. Front: Terry Yorath, Frank Gray, Eddie Gray, Peter Lorimer, Trevor Cherry, Billy Bremner, Allan Clarke.**

1975~Talisman

THE role of talisman in a football team is a strange and difficult-to-define concept.

All teams have had them, indeed they are essential to a successful side. There is no definite position, although they are often strikers who can be relied upon to score goals.

The team just "feels better" when the talisman is on the park. He is the leader, the man who makes the team click.

Andy Gray was Dundee United's talisman in his time at Tannadice. His presence was highly instrumental in the club reaching the 1974 Scottish Cup Final and finishing fourth in the last First Division table in 1974-75. Andy scored goals.

But in September 1975 he was transferred to Aston Villa for £110,000. Robbed of their focus, United had a terrible time in the rest of the 1975-76 season. They won two league games between Gray's departure and mid-February and looked odds-on for relegation. Only a 0-0 draw at Ibrox in the final game saved them from the drop on goal-difference.

■ **Dundee United 1974-75. Back, from left: Jackie Copland, Pat Gardner, Dave Narey, Andy Gray, Hamish McAlpine, Doug Smith, Doug Houston, Andy Rolland, Walter Smith. Front: Duncan McLeod, Graeme Payne, George Fleming, Frank Kopel, Goodham, Iain McDonald, Archie Knox.**

1975~St Mirren's climb begins

ALEX FERGUSON'S evolution as the most successful manager in the history of British football really began in Paisley. He had managed East Stirlingshire for four months, June to October 1974, but it was his transformation of The Buddies that indicated a special talent was emerging.

Fergie was 32 when he took over at Love Street. The team was in the lower reaches of the old Second Division, playing to crowds of around 1,000. In his four years at the club he created a Buddies team that set Scottish football alight.

His first season, 1974-75, was a momentous one. It was the year when league placing in the old two-division format decided where a club would play in the new three-tier set-up. Ferguson achieved sixth place in the Second Division, the last slot in what would give entry to the next season's Division One.

St Mirren went from strength to strength, winning Division 1 in 1976-77 and gaining a deserved reputation for playing attractive attacking football.

But St Mirren became the only club to ever sack Alex Ferguson.

There are conflicting accounts of why this happened. Some reports had it that the dismissal was because of payments Fergie authorised for his players that hadn't been sanctioned by the club's board. Another account claims there had been a breach of contract after Ferguson conducted unauthorised talks with Aberdeen about becoming their manager.

■ **St Mirren, 1975-76. Back, from left: John Mowat, Andy Dunlop, Billy Johnston, John Hunt, Joe Plommer, Alex Beckett, John Hughes. Middle: Walter Borthwick, John Young, Alan Hughes, Peter Leonard, Bobby Reid, Dave McConnell, Billy Stark, Brian Kinnear, Alan Munro, Bert Ferguson, Donny McDowell. Front: Eddie McDonald (trainer), Dave Provan (coach), Derek Hyslop, Jim Campbell, Tony Fitzpatrick, Ian Reid, Jackie McGillivray, Alex Ferguson (manager), Rikki McFarlane (physiotherapist). Trophy: The Renfrewshire Cup.**

1975~Cove ambition

THIS photo shows the 1975 Cove Rangers team that won the Aberdeenshire Amateur Championship. The club would, 44 years later, gain promotion to the Scottish senior leagues.

Every club has ambition. But just hoping things will get better isn't enough. Being backed by efficient off-field organisation isn't enough either. On its own, even success on the pitch isn't enough.

You have to change mindsets at every level throughout the club.

Cove became a Junior team in 1985, then gained entry to the Highland League in 1986. They won it seven times and were runners-up six times.

In 2015, a move to the Balmoral Stadium ensured all the criteria were in place for the next step upwards.

An aggregate 7-0 win over Berwick Rangers in the 2019 play-offs made that step a reality.

The process of starting as an amateur club and moving up might sound simple to those who don't know everything that is involved. But make no mistake about it, Cove's arrival in the pro league system is one of the great feats of modern Scottish football.

Aberdeen was a one-club city from 1903 to 2019, The Dons didn't have a true derby. Now they do.

Don't write off Cove one day challenging for the title of top team in the Granite City.

What's to stop them?

■ **The amateur Cove side of 1975. Back, from left: Ross, Morrice, Joss, Mutch, Rose, Saddler, Nicol. Front: Murdoch, Chrystal, Allan, Skene, Emslie, Mowat.**

1977~The Gerd Müller of Dens Park

I T is a measure of the strength of that season's Division 1 that this team, boasting Gordon Strachan, Tommy Gemmell, Thomson Allan and John MacPhail, could only finish third behind Morton and Hearts in 1977-78.

They did score 91 times in the league, however, with the incredibly prolific Billy Pirie getting 35 goals in 39 league games.

Pirie was his side's equivalent of Gerd "Der Bomber" Müller, scoring 106 goals in 137 games over the course of his four-season Dundee career.

Like the German, he had a gift for goals, always popping up in the right place at the right time.

This wasn't an accident, however. Billy's well-timed runs, which always seemed to get him to the ball in the box ahead of defenders, were the result of a finely-tuned football intelligence.

■ **Dundee FC 1976-77. Back, from left: Wilson Hoggan, Davie Johnston, John Martin, Iain Phillip, Thomson Allan, Bobby Robinson, John MacPhail. Front: Alex Caldwell, Ian Purdie, Bobby Ford, Tommy Gemmell, Gordon Strachan, Billy Pirie.**

1978~Beginnings of the Brown era

CLYDE FC have known many a high and many a low in their long history. This is the team that won the Scottish Second Division in 1977-78 — managed by Craig Brown.

Craig, who has a top-flight champions medal as a player, won with Dundee in 1961-62, was part-time boss of Clyde from 1977 to '86. He was also a primary school head teacher and lecturer in primary education.

He left Clyde to become assistant manager to Scotland boss Andy Roxburgh after the 1986 World Cup Finals.

Elevation to the top job came in 1993 and Craig went on to set the longevity record for Scotland managers, being in charge for 70 games and taking the side to the finals of two major tournaments.

■ **Back, from left: Mark Clougherty, Tommy O'Neill, Brian Kinnear, John Arrol, John Martin, Joe Ward, Neil Hood. Middle: Stewart McMillan (trainer), Ian Henderson, Sandy McNaughton, Jim Nelson, Greig Young, Jim Kean, John Brogan, Bobby Ferris, John Watson (physio). Front: Billy Finlay, Eddie Anderson, Brian Ahern, Craig Brown (manager), Gerry McCabe, Arthur Grant, Gerry Marshall.**

1978~The tragedy of Bobby McKean

THIS 1975 Rangers team includes Bobby McKean, who had been a £50,000 capture from St Mirren the previous year, but who would die in tragic circumstances, aged just 25.

Having told his wife he wouldn't be home on the night of March 14, 1978, he changed his mind, left the function he'd been attending in East Kilbride and drove home in atrociously snowy weather.

Without a key, and unable or unwilling to wake his wife, he drove his car into his garage. At some point during the night, to stay warm, Bobby started the car and switched its heater on. He was found by a family friend the next day, having died, by accident, of carbon monoxide poisoning.

■ Rangers in 1975. Back, from left: Colin Stein, Derek Parlane, Colin Jackson, Donald Hunter, Peter McCloy, Stewart Kennedy, Allister Scott, Tom Forsyth, Martin Henderson. Middle: Tom Craig (physio), Gordon Boyd, Chris Robertson, Alex O'Hara, Alan Boyd, Derek Johnston, Alex Miller, Ally Dawson, David Armour, Ian McDougall, Joe Mason (trainer). Front: Jock Wallace (manager), Tommy McLean, Bobby McKean, Graham Fyfe, Alex McDonald, John Greig (captain), Sandy Jardine, Quinton Young, Eric Morris, Jim Denny, John Hamilton.

1978~The idle idol

THERE aren't many players like Andy Ritchie today. Indeed, there never were many like Andy.

The Morton legend was a magician, a supremely gifted footballer whose first touch was sublime, whose sense of balance on the turn was incredible, whose ability with a dead ball was legendary.

But those gifts also contributed to Andy's weaknesses. The game was easy for him. He was so good he almost didn't have to try. And sometimes he didn't try, or at least not appear to try very hard.

With the stubborn refusal to accept defeat of a Billy Bremner, or the sheer will-to-win of a Bobby Evans, Andy Ritchie might have been one of Scotland's great players.

His highlights reel (if cameras had been around to capture them all) would be jaw-dropping. His lowlights reel, however, would be a very static thing.

He would play 260 games in six seasons for Morton and score 136 goals (many of them spectacular) but was retired by the age of 27.

■ **Morton 1978. Back, from left: Andy Ritchie, Roddy Hutchison, David Rae, Denis Connaghan, Billy Trench, Jim Liddle, Bobby Russell, Ally Scott, Bobby Thomson. Middle: Lindsay Hamilton, Jim McLean, Neil Orr, Charlie Brown, Barrie Evans, Joe McLaughlin, Jim Wilkie, Jim Tolmie, Jim Rooney, Jim Thomas, Eamon Lynch, Willie Gray. Front: Mike Jackson, Jimmy Holmes, Jimmy Millar, Tommy Veitch, John McNeil, Benny Rooney (manager), David Hayes, Danny Docherty, Alan McKeenan, Norman Sutton, Alan McGrain.**

1978~Well ah'm no feart o you, pal

THE union of Scottish midfield grafters, if there were such a thing, would have a motto: "Ah'm no feart o you, pal". It is a trait shared by the great exponents of the art, the likes of Asa Hartford, Dave Mackay and Archie Gemmill.

Stuart Beedie was such a player. He started at Montrose and racked up 600 games for St Johnstone, Dundee United, Hibs, Dunfermline, Dundee, and East Fife before returning to Links Park aged 34.

Stuart was involved in one of Scottish football's most infamous moments. In Graeme Souness's debut as Rangers player-manager in 1986 he was sent off for a kick at Hibs' George McCluskey. But what had made Souness lose his rag was Beedie's welcome-to-Scotland "solid challenge".

Souness was one of the toughest guys to play the game. Part of his effectiveness was the aura he carried. Indeed, as an intelligent footballer, Graeme cultivated this reputation as it overawed lesser players.

But Stuart Beedie wasn't the type to be intimidated. Not a dirty player, but he certainly didn't hold back in a 50-50 no matter the opponent. He rattled into the ex-Liverpool superstar, and Souness reacted. Hibs won that game 2-1.

■ **Montrose 1978. Back, from left: Jimmy McIntosh, Stuart Beedie, Gary Murray, Alex Walker, Jim Moffat, Dennis D'Arcy, Keith Joss, John Sheran, Davie Johnston. Front: Bertie Miller, Malcolm Lowe, Dougie Robb, Bobby Livingstone, Ian Hair, Les Barr, Alex Wright.**

■ **Hibernian 1978-79. Back, from left: Stephen Brown, Brian Fairlie, Gordon Rae, Colin Campbell, Mike McDonald, Jim McArthur, Ally McLeod, Jackie McNamara, Bobby Hutchinson, Gerry O'Brien. Middle: John Lambie (trainer), Alec Edwards, Willie Paterson, Paul McGlinchey, Aitchison, Mack, Craig Paterson, Tony Higgins, Ally Brazil, Pat Carroll, Johnstone, John Fraser (trainer). Front: Arthur Duncan, Leitch, Willie Temperley, John Brownlie, George Stewart, Bobby Smith, Willie Murray, Alex McGhee, Des Bremner, Eddie Turnbull (manager).**

1979~The Best of Hibs

INTO what was largely this Hibs squad (left) walked possibly the most talented footballer ever born in the British Isles, George Best.

The Belfast Boy was, by 1979, aged 33, having left Manchester United five years previously. He played 19 games for Hibs in 1979-80 and three games the following season, scoring three goals in total.

And he certainly swelled the crowd. His home debut against Partick Thistle saw Easter Road welcome a 20,622 attendance in a season that had seen 5,000 crowds. This would have been a fine return on chairman Tom Hart's commitment to paying him £2,000 per game.

But Hibs were relegated during Best's time at the club, with a dismal 18 points from 36 games.

It might be argued that the greatest player ever to play in Scottish football was a Hibs player.

But he didn't do them much good.

1979~On the up

THIS Dundee United squad, indeed the club, hadn't yet won a trophy. But that would change in the next few years under the gimlet eye of manager Jim McLean.

■ Back, from left: Leslie, Dodds, Phillip, Graham, Narey, W. Smith, R. Stewart. Middle: Jim McLean, Reilly, A. Dickson (physio), Craig, Lorimer, Hegarty, Neilson, Kopel, Addison, Milne, Fleming, G. Low (coach), I. Campbell (coach). Front: I. Stewart, Cavanagh, O'Brien, Taylor, Murray, Frye, Holt, Sturrock, Payne, Ballantyne, Kirkwood.

■ As with Dundee United on the previous page, this is a team standing on the brink of greatness. The 1979-80 Dons would usher in a golden era in the club's history. This line-up has quality in every position. Some would spend their entire career at Pittodrie, others would move on. Back, from left: Joe Harper, Alan Oliver, Ian Scanlon, John Hewitt, John Gardiner, Bobby Clark, Jim Leighton, Michael Robertson, Steve Archibald, Derek Hamilton, Mark McGhee.

■ **Middle:** Pat Stanton (asst. manager), Roland Arnott (physio), Neil Cooper, Andy Dornan, Doug Considine, Doug Bell, Willie Garner, Neil Simpson, Alex McLeish, Steve Morrison, Dom Sullivan, Neil Burke, Doug Rougvie, Andy Watson, Lenny Taylor (youth coach), Alex Ferguson (manager). **Front:** Teddy Scott (trainer), George Middleton, John McMaster, Dave Thompson, Drew Jarvie, Chris Slavin, Willie Miller, Tommy Maguire, Gordon Strachan, Ian Angus, Duncan Davidson, Neale Cooper, Stuart Kennedy.

1980~The Fleeting dynasty's progress

THE success of the Fleeting dynasty is a matter of pride in Scotland. Jim, pictured here with the Ayrshire Cup and alongside future Liverpool great Stevie Nicol, was an Ayr United legend in his own right. But he is also the father of, arguably, Scotland's greatest ever female footballer.

Julie Fleeting would bc born four months after this photo was taken. She would grow up to be an Arsenal superstar and is a contender for the title of most natural header of a ball, of either gender, that Scotland has ever produced.

Julie scored 116 goals in 121 games for Scotland, the only British player, so far, to score more than 100 international goals.

■ **Ayr United 1980. Back, from left: Willie McCulloch (second team trainer), Mark Shanks, Billy McColl, Stevie Nicol, David Armour, Stuart Rennie, Ian McAllister, Billy Hendry, Gerry Christie, Eric Morris, Billy Smith (under-18 coach) Front: Willie McLean (manager), Jim McSherry, Robert Connor, Jim Fleeting, Ian Cashmore, Ally Love, Derek Frye, George Caldwell (assistant manager).**

1980~Ian Stewart, lower league football genius

FOOTBALL fans often enjoy discussing a hypothetical question. One of the more common examples crops up when discussing managers of super-rich clubs. We say, "But could they do it on a shoestring budget at a lower-league team?"

And we wonder if the opposite might equally be true: if a man who has consistently over-achieved with minnows was put in charge of a giant of the game, what miracles might he perform?

Ian Stewart was a journeyman winger with several Angus clubs, before becoming player-manager at Brechin City in 1978 and lifting them from their consistent bottom-of-the-pyramid status to be challengers at the other end of the league.

In 1980 he moved to Arbroath. In his very first game he held Alex Ferguson's Aberdeen to a 1-1 draw in the third round of the Scottish Cup. He was sacked three years later, but had narrowly missed promotion two seasons in a row and lost only 39 of 132 league matches.

Then, in seven years at Links Park, he coached Montrose to the first national silverware in the club's 106-year history (see page 222).

So it's a fair question to ask . . . what might Ian Stewart have achieved if he'd been put in charge of Real Madrid?

■ **Ian Stewart's Arbroath team who drew 1-1 with Aberdeen. Back, from left: Lindsay Kydd, Ernie Scrimgeour, Steve Mylles, John Lister, Tom Cargill, Alan McKenzie, Tommy Yule. Front: Wilson Stark, David Durno, Billy Gavine, Billy Wells, Charlie Barbour, Terry Wilson.**

1980~Donald McKay and his Bonnie Dundee

DON McKAY had been a goalkeeper with Dundee's rivals United for 10 years in the 1960s, but had been away from the city for almost a decade before a surprise return to Dens Park to replace outgoing manager Tommy Gemmell.

But McKay hadn't been wasting his time, he had been learning the art of management by first coaching the Bristol City youths, then as boss of Norresundby in Denmark. Like Ian Stewart on the previous page, he had become a wily club manager.

His appointment sparked an upsurge in the fortunes of a club that had been yo-yoing between the Premier League and Division One. Within months he got the Dark Blues to the League Cup Final, the first lower league club to reach a final for 17 years, and finished the season by pipping St Johnstone to the Division One second spot behind Hibs.

In his three years as Dundee boss McKay made up-and-coming star Iain Ferguson a regular starter, signed fans' favourite Cammy Fraser from Hearts and got the best out of Dee stalwarts like Bobby Glennie and George McGeachie.

■ **Dundee 1979-80. Back, from left: Jocky Scott, Willie Watson, Ian McDougall, Ally Donaldson, Bobby Geddes, Brian Scrimgeour, Les Barr, Alex Caldwell. Middle: Eric Ferguson (physio), Erich Schaedler, Mark McGhee, Stuart McLaren, Alan Lamb, Peter Millar, George McCeachie, Billy Williamson, Stuart Turnbull, Jimmy Murphy. Front: Willie Wallace (coach), Ian Redford, John McPhail, Eric Sinclair, Iain Ferguson, Bobby Glennie, Stephen McIntosh, Jim Shirra, John Bradley, Hugh Robertson (coach).**

203

1981~Sandy, a man who knows the game

THERE are people who have vast experience and are, quite rightly, respected because of that by those in the game. Though this expertise is sometimes undervalued by punters.

Sandy Clark was born in Airdrie and signed for his home town club in 1974. He went on to have a lengthy playing career, at six different clubs, with many a high and low along the way. All the time, he was gathering a precious commodity — knowledge.

Since finishing playing in 1990, Sandy has been almost continually employed as a coach and manager.

This speaks volumes not only for his playing and coaching talents, but also for that in-depth and hard-won education he has gained. There is simply no substitute for experience.

Sandy is now among the most

respected and knowledgable figures within the Scottish game.

Experience in football is always a valuable thing.

■ **Airdrieonians 1981. Back, from left: George Anderson, Harry Cairney, Tommy Black, Frank Close, Alan Davidson, Ian Gordon, Albert Burnett, Kevin Farrell, John Flood. Middle: Unknown coach, Harry Erwin, Tommy McCafferty, Jim March, Dave Thomson, John Martin, Colin Campbell, Stewart Miller, Arthur McKay, Jim Kerr, Wilson Humphries. Front: Billy Reid (coach), Bobby Watson (manager), Willie McGuire, Tommy Walker, Norrie Anderson, Pat McCluskey, Sandy Clark, Brian McKeown, Jim Rodger, Steve Richardson, Billy Ramsey.**

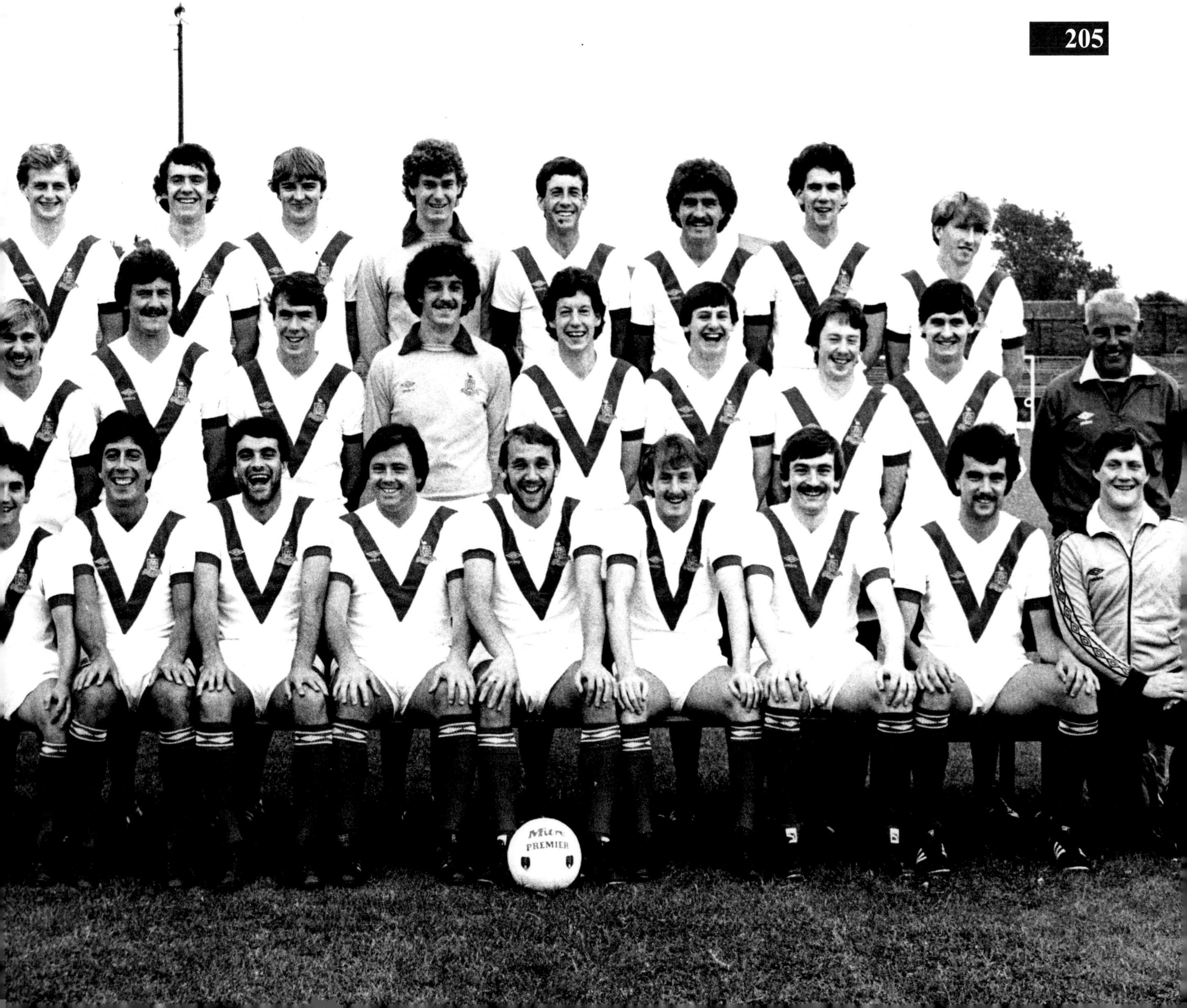
Mitre
PREMIER

1981~Bud always enjoyed himself

WILLIE JOHNSTON, known to team-mates as Bud, was quite a guy. He had great skill, world-class pace, was a powerful header of a ball, and had a natural footballing brain. He also had a quick temper, being sent off more than 20 times during his lengthy career.

One of his perceived misdemeanours, however, was entirely undeserved. Taking pills for hay fever at World Cup Argentina '78 should never have resulted in a drugs ban and a ridculous media witch-hunt.

Willie liked a laugh. His repertoire of japes and jokes, is the stuff of legend. He tells the story himself of negotiating the purchase of a greenhouse from a fan over the course of taking several corners for West Brom.

His TV interviews could have been mistaken for stand-up comedy routines.

In this photo, taken during Johnston's second spell at Ibrox, he is shouting at the cameraman and most of his team-mates are grinning at whatever joke it was that he had just cracked. Bud had a huge amount of skill and an equally big personality.

■ **Middle:** A. Anderson, J. McIntyre, Graham Watson, Gordon Dalziel, Ian Redford, Derek Johnstone, Jim Bett, Doug Robertson, Kenny Lyall, Alex Forsyth, Kenny Black, Stuart Hogg.
Front: Manager John Greig, Tommy McLean, Billy MacKay, Billy Davies, Bobby Russell, Ally Dawson, Sandy Jardine, Davie Cooper, John McDonald, Willie Johnston, Joe Mason.

1981~Scots punch above their weight

THERE is always a special feeling of pride when a Scottish club pulls off a result that resonates across the continent.

Dundee United's 5-0 victory over Borussia Monchengladbach in the UEFA Cup in 1981 was one of many times Scots clubs have made Europe take notice.

As a nation, we have regularly punched above our weight.

The Germans had been finalists the previous season, boasted a young Lothar Matthaus in their midfield, and had Frank Mill, who would get a 1990 World Cup winners' medal, up front.

Borussia had won the away leg 2-0. But the Tangerines, roared on by a 16,000 crowd, took them apart at Tannadice in the second round tie on November 3, 1981.

Scorers were Milne (36 min.), Kirkwood (44), Sturrock (57), Hegarty (75), and Bannon (76).

The fifth goal, a run from the half-way line, leaving defenders trailing in his wake, and a cool finish by Eamonn Bannon, has gone down in history as one of United's greatest ever moments.

■ **The team that played that night in 1981. Back, from left: John Holt, Derek Murray, Billy Kirkwood, Paul Hegarty. Front: Dave Narey, Paul Sturrock, Richard Gough, Eamonn Bannon, Hamish McAlpine, Davie Dodds, Ralph Milne.**

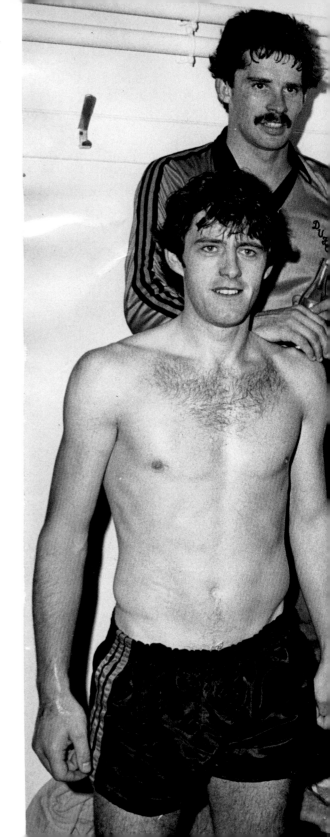

1981~Tony Higgins, man of the people and unsung hero

FEW terrace chants were ever sung in praise of Tony Higgins. His playing style might have been described by a cruel man as "gangly".

Tony played in the midfields of Hibs, Partick Thistle, Morton and Stranraer in the '70s and '80s, racking up more than 200 games before injury ended his career in 1987. But he rarely features in discussions of Scotland's great players.

However, Tony was, and still is, a true man of the people.

He took over the chairmanship of the Scottish Professional Footballers' Association Scotland from Alex Ferguson and fought for his members. When a player has a grievance, or isn't being treated in a fair manner, it is the PFAS that stands up for him.

Tony was raised discussing socialist politics at home and carried those values on into his professional life.

He later became Scotland's representative of FIFPro, the international footballers' union, and Tony has played a prominent role in setting up players' unions in Africa.

For a time he even contemplated leaving football to run for election as an MP. It wouldn't have been the Tories that Tony would have stood for.

Tony is an unsung hero of the Scottish, and world, game. His name deserves to be chanted.

■ **Partick Thistle 1981. Back, from left: Dave McKinnon, Iain Jardine, Tony Higgins, Frank Welsh, Kenny Watson, Alex O'Hara. Middle: John Lapsley, Joe Sweeney, Andy Anderson, Alan Rough, Dougie McNab, Jackie Campbell, Brian Whittaker. Front: Peter Cormac (manager), Ian McDonald, Willie Gibson, Donald Park, George Clark, Jamie Doyle, Donnie McKinnon (physio).**

211

1982~Mystery of Motherwell

IT is one of the mysteries of Scottish football — why didn't the tremendous Motherwell team that won the Division One title so comprehensively in 1981-82, go on to much greater things?

The title had been won at a canter, with Davie Hay's side leaving Kilmarnock and Hearts 10 and 11 points behind. Hay left for a job in the USA, but the new boss, Jock Wallace, certainly knew what it took to be a winner in Scotland and had the wily Frank Connor alongside him in the dugout.

Among the ranks were Brian McClair, who would go on to be a Celtic and Manchester United legend, Alex Forsyth, who had already played more than 100 games for Man U, a youthful Gary McAllister, the highly

entertaining Brian McLaughlin, who had been the Division One players' player of the year and the much-travelled Alfie Conn Jr.

In the October of 1982, the made-of-iron Ally Mauchlen would arrive from Kilmarnock, further strengthening the side.

One of the great characters of Scottish football, Hugh (Shuggie) Sproat, was in the goal . . . and would sometimes swing on the crossbar to amuse the fans!

The talented John Gahagan and Ian Clinging were pushing through, and big Steve McLelland, who had starred as a sweeper in Division One, was about to become a centre-forward (much to his surprise).

This squad was multi-talented. So quite how it managed to finish one place above the relegation

places in 82-83 is a puzzle for all 'Well fans.

But then, every club's fans can point to a line-up that should have done better. It is one of the enduring frustrations of football.

■ **Motherwell 1982-83. Back, from left: Willie Irvine, Bruce Cleland, Brian Coyne, Hugh Sproat, Graeme Forbes, James Burns, Desmond Healy. Middle: Tom O'Hara, Ian Clinging, Alfie Conn, Alex Forsyth, Joe Carson, Brian McClair, Gary McAllister, Stephen McLelland. Front: John McKay, John Gahagan, Willie McKenzie (trainer), Jock Wallace (manager), Frank Connor (assistant manager), Dave Milne (physiotherapist), Stuart Rafferty, Brian McLaughlin.**

1983~Sir Alex's best achievement

SIR Alex Ferguson's achievements with Manchester United are world-renowned. But football expects Man U to be successful. The greatest illustration of his talent for management was to make a club from Scotland's third largest city into the best in the country — and by a good margin. He then beat Bayern Munich and Real Madrid while winning the European Cup-Winners' Cup. Of everything Fergie did in football, this was his finest hour.

■ **Aberdeen 1983-84. Back, from left: L. Taylor (youth coach), Willie Falconer, Doug Bell, Ian Downie, Steven Smith, Derek Hamilton, Ian Angus, Ian Robertson, Steve Gray, David Lawrie, Tommy McIntyre, Billy Stark, G. Adams (youth coach). Middle: Alex Stephen, Gary Riddell, Neil Simpson, Steve Cowan, John McGachie, Bryan Gunn, Jim Leighton, Alex McLeish, Brian Mitchell, Doug Rougvie, John Boag, Paul Wright, Teddy Scott (trainer). Front: D. Wylie (physio), Neale Cooper, Ian Porteous, John Hewitt, Eric Black, Mark McGhee, Alex Ferguson (manager), Willie Miller, Stuart Kennedy, John McMaster, Gordon Strachan, Peter Weir, Archie Knox (asst. manager). Trophies: Aberdeenshire Cup, European Cup-Winners' Cup, Scottish Cup.**

1983~Super-Ally McCoist, the man who guaranteed goals

ALLY McCOIST is a multi-talented man. Probably the most rounded football media personality that Scotland has ever produced. He has a knack for a pithy or funny line but when working as a summariser his assessments of tactical game play are insightful and intelligent.

His ready laugh and affable nature make him very good at "TV stuff".

While he is an engaging figure on our screens, broadcasting is not what he was best at.

His greatest talent over his career has been his ability to do the most difficult job in football — to put the ball in the net.

In 100 years' time, Rangers supporters will still be talking about his goalscoring feats.

He is Rangers' greatest ever scorer, with 355 goals. He holds the club records for League, League Cup, and European goals scored. He is also third on the list of all-time Rangers appearances.

His period as manager came at a difficult time for the club but at all times he conducted himself with dignity, and his desire to do what was best for Rangers, never himself, was always apparent.

It is not in the Scottish nature to become sentimental even over the greatest heroes of our national game. So it is sad, but likely true,

to suggest that the magnificent playing achievements of Alastair Murdoch McCoist won't be fully appreciated until he is gone.

One day, there will be statues erected to Ally.

■ **Rangers 1983-84. Back, from left: Dave MacKinnon, Ally Dawson, Ally McCoist, Robert Prytz. Middle: Ian Redford, Gregor Stevens, Craig Paterson, Peter McCloy, Dave McPherson, Sandy Clark, Davie Cooper. Front: Kenny Lyall, John MacDonald, John McClelland, Billy Davies, Bobby Russell.**

1983~One game can turn an entire season

WHEN Dundee United won the league in 1982-83, they did it with a team that had talent in all departments, and a brilliant — if sometimes inexplicably angry — manager in Jim McLean.

Championships aren't ever won in just one game. But one game can have a defining effect on a championship.

Late in that season, United were in contention for the league but never favourites, until they went to Celtic Park on Wedneday, April 20, 1983. The Tangerines won 3-2, despite having Richard Gough sent off early in the second half. McLean hailed it his team's best-ever away result.

The following Saturday, Aberdeen beat Celtic 1-0 at Pittodrie, while United thrashed Kilmarnock 4-0.

These results left United requiring three wins in three games to guarantee the title — which they achieved in style with 4-0 wins over Motherwell and Morton and a 2-1 final day beating of Dundee.

■ **Dundee United with the 1982-83 Championship trophy. Back, from left: Davie Dodds, Alex Taylor, John Clark, Hamish McAlpine, John Holt, Dave Narey, Richard Gough, Derek Stark. Front: Ralph Milne, Paul Hegarty, Billy Kirkwood, Maurice Malpas, Eamonn Bannon.**

1985~The first step on Andy's long, long road

THEY always say that if a player is good enough, he's old enough — so the reverse must also be true. If a player is good enough, he's young enough.

Central defender Andy Millen was always good enough, wherever he went. He proved it by playing, with distinction, until he was 45. Andy was adept at managing a game while he was on the pitch. That might sound simple but if you know your football, you'll recognise it as a rare skill.

This photo shows him at the start of his career, a laddie with the Perth Saintees. After that, he went on quite a journey. In order, his clubs were: St Johnstone, Alloa, Hamilton Accies, Kilmarnock, Ipswich, Hibs, Raith Rovers, Ayr United, Greenock Morton, Clyde, St Mirren and Queen's Park. He played well over 800 games in total.

He's the oldest outfield player in the SPL era, appearing for St Mirren against Hearts at 42 years, 279 days.

His last game, for Queen's Park, was at the age of 45.

■ St Johnstone 1985. Back, from left: Kenny Lyall, Gordon Drummond, Dougie Barron, John Balavage, Frank Liddell. Middle: Charlie Bates (physio), Drew Rutherford, Denis McDaid, Joe Reid, Gordon Winter, Sammy Johnston, Joe McGurn, Derek Addison, Athol Henderson (coach). Front row, left to right; Jim Morton, Andy Millen, Ian Gibson (player-manager), David Williamson, Eddie McGonigle.

1985~Champions after 106 years

D OUG SOMNER was 33 by the time he arrived at Links Park in 1984, and had enjoyed a lengthy and productive career.
He played for, and scored a lot of goals for, Partick Thistle, had grabbed St Mirren's first-ever European goal and been awarded three Scottish League XI caps. He was the Premier League's top scorer of 1979-80 while with The Buddies.

Doug became the Montrose talisman in the memorable 1984-85 Second Division season, in which the club won their first national silverware after fully 106 years of existence.

Ian Stewart (see also page 200) crafted a team that included former Dundee full-back Les Barr in his second spell at Links Park, one-time Stoke City starlet Steve Lennox, the inimitable Chic McLelland, and the solid Martin Allan, John Sheran and Neil Forbes. They were a braw team.

■ **Montrose 1985. Back, from left: Ian Stewart (manager), Gary Loch, Mark Bennett, Doug Somner, Tony Duffy, Ray Charles, Neil Forbes, Steve Lennox, Ronnie Cusiter, John Sheran, Neil Burke. Front: Colin O'Brien, Alex Wright, Les Barr, Chic McLelland, Martin Allan, Martin Caithness, Dougie Robb.**

1986~Revolution

IT is impossible to underplay the effect that the 1986 arrival of Graeme Souness had on Scottish football.

He reversed the 100-year-old drain of talent, bringing English stars to Scotland instead of the other way round. He famously signed Maurice Johnston, and put in place the foundations upon which Rangers' nine-in-a-row dominance would be built.

But he also had an effect on every other team in the land.

Celtic had to react to the new order. After a few years they swept out their old-fashioned business model and emerged with a new, professional approach.

Every other Scottish club with ambition started to look abroad for players, with the costs and the advantages (and the many disadvantages) that would bring.

Though a stellar player, Scottish football probably didn't see Souness's best form on the pitch. He played 50 games and confirmed his status as a ferocious tackler, but his very best playing days were at Liverpool.

His conduct off the field, though, was hugely impressive.

He was diplomatic but forceful, he was dignified yet retained his fierce will to win. In many ways, he revived the ethos of Bill Struth. Thinking big but with attention to detail, demanding victory and insisting there could be no dispute over who deserved to win.

Souness stayed less than five years at Ibrox but his legacy would last for decades.

■ Rangers, Skol Cup winners 1988. Back, from left: Graeme Souness, Ian Ferguson, John Brown, Ally McCoist, Gary Stevens, Derek Ferguson, physio Phil Boersma, Richard Gough, Jimmy Nicholl, Kevin Drinkell, Walter Smith. Front: Terry Butcher, Stuart Munro, Chris Woods, Mark Walters, Ray Wilkins, Neale Cooper.

1986~The pain that injuries will bring

THROUGHOUT this book, you'll find the names of men whose promising careers were cut short through no fault of their own. Injuries take a toll of footballers.

Lex Baillie looked like he was on his way to becoming a regular with Celtic, and was on the winning side in two Old Firm matches in 1987-88.

But, struggling with ligament damage, he was transferred to St Mirren in 1991 then signed for Dunfermline. A commanding centre-half, Lex's undoubted talent deserved more than retiral from the game at age 28. He did, however, carve out a successful career in the police force after his playing days.

■ Celtic 1986. Back, from left: Lex Baillie, Roy Aitken, Alan McInally, Bob Latchford, Pat Bonner, Pierce O'Leary, Derek Whyte, Paul McGugan. Middle: Davie Hay (manager), Jim Steel (physio), Mark Smith, John Traynor, Tony Shepherd, Doug McGuire, Ronnie Coyle, Paul Chalmers, Sandy Fraser, Stephen Kean, Anton Rogan, Brian McGhee, John Kelman, Bryan Scott. Front: Bobby Lennox (coach), Maurice Johnston, Davie Provan, Mark McGhee, Willie McStay, Paul McStay, Danny McGrain, Murdo MacLeod, Brian McClair, Peter Grant, Tommy Burns, Owen Archdeacon.

1987~A superstar of the game ...with demons troubling him

FRANK McGARVEY was a major star of the game in Scotland in the 1970s and '80s. He became the hottest property in St Mirren's team under Alex Ferguson, scoring hatfuls of goals as the club stormed to the Division One title playing an attacking, exciting brand of football.

This led to Bob Paisley's Liverpool paying £270,000 for him in 1979. But, unable to settle on Merseyside and frustrated at a lack of first-team opportunities, 10 months later Celtic broke the Scottish football transfer record to bring him back north of the Border, for £250,000.

They got their money's worth. Celtic would win two league championships, two Scottish Cups and a League Cup in the five years that they had the energetic McGarvey leading the line.

He returned to St Mirren, where his drive and talent helped the Buddies to their Scottish Cup win of 1987.

But like many a Scottish player before and after him, he had off-field troubles.

Frank didn't hide on the pitch and didn't hide when it came to talking about his demons.

As he revealed in his searingly honest autobiography, *Totally Frank*, he was hopelessly addicted to gambling. He lost his home and his marriage and at one point admits to contemplating taking his own life. He fought back, though it was a hard road, and after retiring became a joiner and flooring expert.

Footballers aren't normal people. They are heroes, above the normal run of mankind — which is a double-edged sword.

Frank remains a revered figure among St Mirren and Celtic supporters. Fans always remember their heroes and, no matter what his troubles may have been, Frank McGarvey's goalscoring skills ensure he will always be a hero.

■ **St Mirren's Scottish Cup-winning side of 1987, with Frank in the middle holding the trophy.**

1987~United's conveyor belt

JIM McLEAN had an eye for football talent second to none. This 1987-88 squad (just after the club reached the UEFA Cup Final) illustrates his Dundee United conveyor belt.

Alongside the first-team men (10 of the club's all-time top 20 appearance-makers are in this photo) are the kids coming through. Billy McKinlay, Paddy Connolly, Alex Cleland, Ray McKinnon, Allan Preston, Brian Welsh, Gordon McLeod, and Scott Thomson would all go on to have lengthy careers in the game.

■ **Back, from left: French, Brennan, McAdams, Redford, B. Thomson, Beaumont, S. Thomson, Welsh, Clark. Third row: Curran, McKinnon, Kinnaird, J. McLeod, G. McLeod, Connolly, Page, McKinlay, Gallacher. Second row: Ronald, Bremner, Bowman, Preston, Ferguson, Kopel, McGinnis, Bishop, McInally, Cleland, Irvine. Front: Manager Jim McLean, physio Jim Joyce, Malpas, Kirkwood, Hegarty, Narey, Sturrock, Holt, Bannon, coaches G. Wallace, I. Campbell.**

231

1987~Boys of the Vale

HUTCHISON VALE Youth Football Club, with its excellent coaching, has produced an astonishing amount of players who have gone on to have successful senior careers.

Five Hibs players in this photo came through Vale's ranks: Eddie May, Peter Cormack, Micky Weir, Danny Lennon and John Collins.

■ **Hibs 1987. Back, from left: Callum Milne, Alan Sneddon, Tommy McIntyre, Gordon Chisholm, Allan Rough, Gordon Hunter, Findlay, Graham Mitchell, Pat McGinley. Middle: Joe Tortolano, Eddie May, Paul McGovern, Allan Peters, A. Hart, K. Waugh, G. Cowan, David Fellinger, Willie Miller, Paul Kane, Bobby Smith. Front: Alex Miller, Peter Cormack, Micky Weir, Danny Lennon, Steve Cowan, Gordon Rae, George McCluskey, John Collins, Joe McBride, A. Stevenson, M. Ferguson.**

1991~Well's name was on the cup

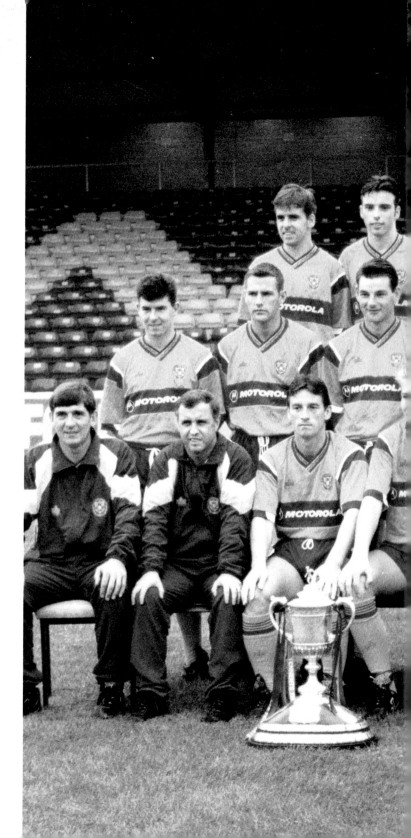

THE best cup final, perhaps of all time, came after one of the best cup runs of all time. The old saying "their name was on the cup from the start" was never more true than in 1991.

The Steelmen beat Aberdeen at Pittodrie in the Third Round, were taken to penalties by Morton in the quarter-final, then saw off Celtic 4-2 in a replayed semi-final before winning by the odd goal in seven against Dundee United in the final.

The old steel town had never seen such a party as that night's party.

■ **Motherwell ready for the 1991-92 season. Back, from left: Paul Burke, Alex Burns, Scott Kinross, Jim Brown, Iain Ferguson, Bobby Russell, Colin O'Neill, Mark Dickson, Stevie Bryce. Middle: Jamie Dolan, Jim Gardner, John Philliben, Stevie Kirk, Jamie Picken, Robert Maaskant, Billy Thomson, Luc Nijholt, Phil O'Donnell, Ian Angus, Jim Griffin. Front: Tom Forsyth, Tommy McLean, Dougie Arnott, Bart Verheul, Davie Cooper, Chris McCart, Paul McGrillen, Tony Shepherd, Joe McLeod, Bobby Holmes, Bobby Jenkins.**

1991~Support your home town team

IT's easy to follow a successful club. Trophies, cup finals and European jaunts give supporters opportunities to celebrate and feel good.

Some clubs rarely win national honours or campaign in foreign lands.

But that doesn't make them less worthy of support. Nor does it mean that their fans are less loyal, or don't feel the sting of defeat so keenly.

It is an enduring, repetitive travesty that the national media show little interest in smaller clubs, instead focusing on the sometimes trivial minutiae involving the "big boys".

A supporter loves his or her team no matter what. Through success and failure, good times and bad.

But which is "your" team?

Many supporters' choice is passed on as a family tradition, but if it ever comes to choosing a team, then surely the only thing to do is to follow your local team. Not one from a city far away, not the currently most successful team in the land.

There is honour in supporting the team based where you live. A town's football club is part of that town's identity, part of your identity. When the club has success, the whole community takes pride in itself.

So we end this book with a simple message — support your local team.

Football as we know it will die if the nation doesn't have a healthy league system.

The line-ups of all teams, giants and minnows, are what makes this book a book.

■ Cowdenbeath's Division Two promotion-winning team 1991-92: Back, from left: John Sharp, Hugh Douglas, Paul Johnston, John Wright, Neil Irvine, Eric Archibald, Billy Lamont, Dave McGovern, Andy Irving, David Taylor, Willie Syme, coach. Front: Jimmy Reekie, Colin Scott, Sandy Robertson, Graham Buckley, John Brownlie (manager), Billy Bennett, Kevin Hamill, Scott Fraser, Scott Ferguson.

■ **Dumbarton 1934, players only. Back, from left: William McDonald, Martin Watson, William Simpson, George Taylor, Charles Ballantyne, Dick Ritchie. Front: Richard English, John Wallace, Johnny Haddow, Thomas Cumming, Robert Henderson.**

INDEX

■ **Stenhousemuir 1930. Back, from left: J. Walker, D. Connelly, J. Murdoch, T. Jack, J. W. Brown, James Jessiman. Front: W. Knox, J. Sutton, J. Allison, James Turnbull, L. Robertson.**

If you liked this book, you'll love...

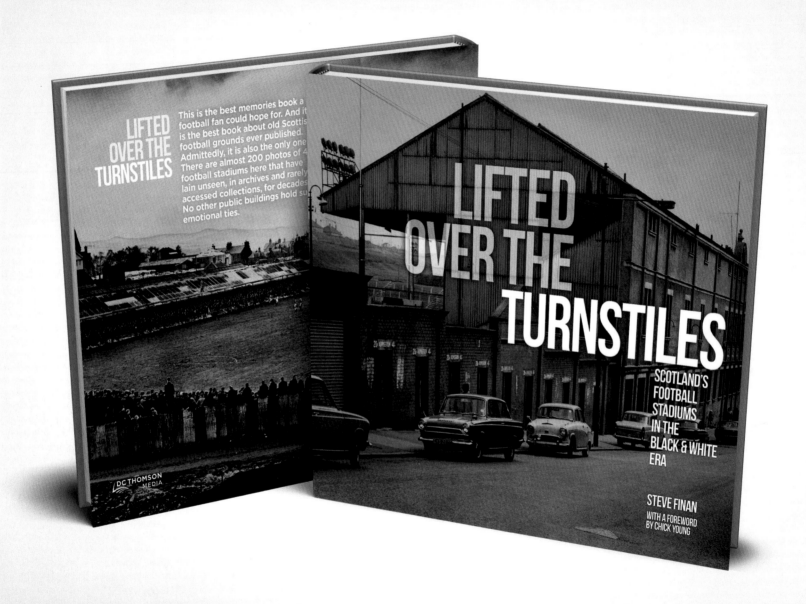

www.dcthomsonshop.co.uk